Listening 2

# CAMBRIDGE SKILLS FOR FLUENCY

*Cambridge Skills for Fluency* is a series of supplementary materials covering the skills of listening, speaking, reading and writing; each skill is developed at four levels, from pre-intermediate through to advanced.

The series aims to develop students' confidence and fluency in English, by offering a variety of topics and activities which engage students' interest and encourage them to share their personal reactions and opinions.

Although all the books in the series share the same underlying principles, we have tried to avoid complete uniformity across the series, and so each book has its own features and its own particular approach to skills development:
- The *Listening* books aim to develop students' ability to understand real-life spoken English, through recordings of natural, spontaneous speech, selected and edited to make them accessible at each level.
- The *Speaking* books aim to develop oral fluency by focusing on topics that are personally relevant to students and which encourage students to draw on their own life experience, feelings and cultural knowledge.
- The *Reading* books aim to develop students' skill in reading English by introducing them to a wide variety of authentic texts, supported by tasks and activities designed to increase involvement and confidence in the reading process.
- The *Writing* books place writing in a central position in the language class, presenting it as a creative activity which contributes to language learning in general.

Level 2 of the series consists of the following titles:
*Listening 2* by Adrian Doff and Carolyn Becket
*Speaking 2* by Joanne Collie and Stephen Slater
*Reading 2* by Simon Greenall and Diana Pye
*Writing 2* by Andrew Littlejohn

CAMBRIDGE SKILLS FOR FLUENCY

Series Editor: Adrian Doff

# Listening 2

*Adrian Doff*
*Carolyn Becket*

CAMBRIDGE
UNIVERSITY PRESS

PUBLISHED BY THE PRESS SYNDICATE OF THE UNIVERSITY OF CAMBRIDGE
The Pitt Building, Trumpington Street, Cambridge, United Kingdom

CAMBRIDGE UNIVERSITY PRESS
The Edinburgh Building, Cambridge CB2 2RU, UK
40 West 20th Street, New York, NY 10011–4211, USA
10 Stamford Road, Oakleigh, VIC 3166, Australia
Ruiz de Alarcón 13, 28014 Madrid, Spain
Dock House, The Waterfront, Cape Town 8001, South Africa

http://www.cambridge.org

© Cambridge University Press 1991

First published 1991
Eighth printing 1999

Printed in the United Kingdom at the University Press, Cambridge

ISBN 0 521 36748 4 book
ISBN 0 521 36545 7 set of 2 cassettes

GO

# Contents

# Thanks

We are very grateful to the following people who have helped in developing this book:
- Our editors, Jeanne McCarten, Lindsay White and Alison Silver.
- Peter Taylor, of Taylor Riley Productions Ltd, and Studio AVP of London for their advice and assistance with the recordings, and for producing the final cassette.
- Teachers and students at the Edinburgh Language Foundation and the Institute of Applied Language Studies, Edinburgh, for their help in arranging and taking part in recordings.

We would like to thank the following people who have contributed to the recordings:

Richard Conte
David Crosbie
Bryan Cruden
Julie Darling
Donna Dimambro
Sue Evans
Colette Fitzpatrick
Stella Forge
Emma Henly
Tony Jemmett
Christopher Jones
Josephine Jones
Marie Anne Julian
Kate Lawrence
Claire MacGregor

Alejandro Mendes
Andre Meyer
Nan Mulder
Louisa Preskett
Nicola Preskett
Patrick Rayner
Anna Ross
Cathy Rylance
Diana Seaville
Olga Taxidou
Doreen Taylor
Hilary Walston
Ronald Wilcox
Kit Woods

# Map of the book

| Unit | Functional areas | Vocabulary areas | Listening strategies |
|---|---|---|---|
| 1 Music in the mind | Imagining scenes; remembering scenes. | Music. | Forming a mental picture. |
| 2 Strangers in the street | Requests; agreeing and refusing; asking personal information. | Buying and selling; food and drink. | Preparing an appropriate response. |
| 3 Embarrassing moments | Narration. | Visitors; dogs; shops; embarrassment. | Following a story; predicting and guessing. |
| 4 Conversations in public | Making enquiries; giving directions; 'small talk'. | Travel; public places; parties. | Listening against background noise; preparing an appropriate response. |
| 5 Views | Describing scenes. | Cities; landscapes. | Forming a mental picture. |
| 6 On the line | Making arrangements; 'small talk'. | Answerphones; friends. | Listening for specific information. |
| 7 Intruders | Narration. | Fears and phobias; crime. | Predicting and guessing; following a story. |
| 8 Childhood | Narration; describing a process. | Childhood; accidents; games. | Following a story; following an explanation. |
| 9 Bought and sold | Describing objects. | Buying and selling; household objects. | Listening for specific information; following the 'thread' of a conversation. |
| 10 Behind the picture | Describing the past; describing a scene; interpreting a picture. | The past; homes; art. | Matching with your own interpretation. |

| Unit | | Functional areas | Vocabulary areas | Listening strategies |
|------|--|------------------|------------------|---------------------|
| 11 | Believe it or not | Giving explanations; making deductions. | Superstitions; fortune telling. | Following an explanation; matching with your own beliefs. |
| 12 | Bread and mushrooms | Describing a process; describing features. | Food; cookery; the natural world. | Following an explanation; listening for specific information. |
| 13 | Learning to draw | Giving an explanation; giving instructions. | Personality; art; the mind. | Matching with your own beliefs; following instructions. |
| 14 | Male and female | Giving an explanation; recounting experiences. | Male and female roles; children. | Matching with your own beliefs/ experience. |
| 15 | Bees | Describing activities; describing a process. | Beekeeping; clothes and equipment. | Matching against previous knowledge; predicting and guessing. |
| 16 | Emergency | Giving instructions; narration. | Illness; emergencies. | Matching against previous knowledge; following a story; predicting and guessing. |
| 17 | Punishing children | Giving an explanation; expressing opinions. | Punishment; parents and children; calligraphy. | Matching with your own beliefs/ experience. |
| 18 | Planet Earth | Making predictions; agreeing and disagreeing. | Traffic in cities; the world; the environment. | Following an argument; matching with your own opinions. |
| 19 | Sporting moments | Narration; giving a commentary. | Sport; outdoor activities. | Listening for main points; following rapid speech. |
| 20 | War zones | Describing scenes; describing lifestyles. | War; travel; politics. | Forming a mental picture; matching with your own beliefs. |

# 1 | Music in the mind

## A Mental images

1   ▭ You will hear a piece of music. What images come into your mind as you listen to it?

Write down three words that represent what you see in your mind.

2   ▭ You will hear five people saying what images they see as they listen to the music.

Listen and write down three *key words* from each description (the three words that seem most important).

1 .................................................

2 .................................................

3 .................................................

4 .................................................

5 .................................................

Show them to another student. Do you agree what the three words should be?

What country do you think each speaker sees in his/her mind?

3   Now show your own words to another student. Describe the mental picture you saw as you listened to the music.

4   What country do you think this music really comes from?

# B Musical memories

1   📼 You will hear two people describing favourite pieces of music:
Beethoven's 4th Piano Concerto and James Taylor's 'First of May'.
Listen to the music, and to the beginning of what they say.
How is the music connected with the two pictures?

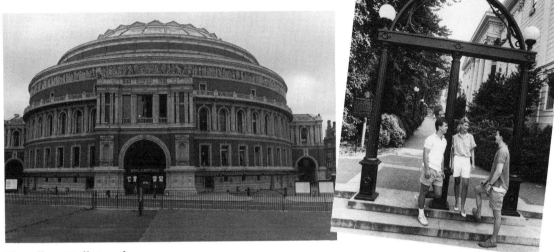

*The Albert Hall, London*

*Athens, Georgia, University campus*

2   The speakers go on to describe their memories of the two places. Which of
the descriptions below do you think belongs to each memory?

|  | Albert Hall | Athens, Georgia |
|---|---|---|
| People wandering around |  |  |
| People holding hands |  |  |
| People swimming |  |  |
| Blue sky |  |  |
| People throwing paper aeroplanes |  |  |
| People throwing footballs |  |  |
| People lying down with newspapers over their faces |  |  |
| Music drifting upwards |  |  |

📼 Now listen and check your answers.

3   Think about the last time you went to a concert. How well does it fit the
description of the Albert Hall? What differences were there?

Imagine the scene in your home town on 1st May. How well would it fit the
description of Athens, Georgia? What differences would there be?

4   **Extension**   Work with another student. Do you have a favourite piece
of music which has specially strong memories for you? Tell your partner
about it.

11

# 2 | Strangers in the street

## A Excuse me . . .

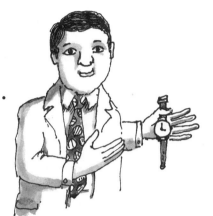

1   Imagine the people in the pictures come up to you in the street. What do you think they might say?

2   Listen to the four remarks on the tape. Imagine that a stranger says these things to you in the street. Think of a suitable reply to each remark and write it down.

3   Now listen to the replies. Were they similar to yours?

4   Listen to the complete conversations and discuss the questions below.

1 Do you think the man is telling the truth?
   Does he seem to you: polite? friendly? rather 'pushy'? rude?
   Would you: look at the watch? buy it? walk away?

2 Do you think the man is telling the truth?
   Does he seem to you: rather aggressive? rather shy? quite normal?
   How much money would you give the man? Why?

3 Does International Aid sound like a useful organisation to you?
   How much money would you give? Why?

4 Which of these words best describe the man's approach: open and friendly? honest and straightforward? aggressive? polite?
   Would you agree to answer the questions?

5   **Extension**   Think of a question that you might ask a stranger in the street (some kind of help, a favour, money, information – anything you like). Think of the best way to ask the question in English, and write it down.

Imagine you are all strangers in the street. Ask other students your question, and respond to their questions.

# B Fast food survey

1   The pictures show some common kinds of fast food in Britain. Which are also common in your own country?
    What other kinds of fast food are common in your country?
    Make a list and then compare it with another student.

2   [cassette] You will hear a market researcher asking someone questions about fast food. Listen to the man's answers and complete the questionnaire.

---

1   Do you ever eat fast food?        Yes ☐        No ☐

2   What kind of fast food do you normally eat?

    1 ..............................................................        3 ..............................................................

    2 ..............................................................        4 ..............................................................

3   How often do you eat fast food?
        every day ☐        more than once a week ☐        less than once a week ☐

4   What time of day do you eat fast food?
        in the morning ☐        in the afternoon ☐
        around midday ☐        in the evening ☐

5   Do you eat fast food as:        a main meal? ☐        a snack between meals? ☐

6   Which of these statements about fast food do you think are true?
    *(Mark the scale: 3 = Yes, 2 = Maybe/Not sure, 1 = No)*

|   | 3 | 2 | 1 |
|---|---|---|---|
| • It's convenient. | | | |
| • It tastes good. | | | |
| • It's good for you. | | | |
| • It's an expensive way of eating. | | | |
| • It creates litter. | | | |

---

3   Work with another student. Discuss how you would answer the questions.

4   **Extension**   Work in pairs. Write a similar questionnaire of your own to find out about people's eating habits. Then use it to ask other students questions.

# 3 | Embarrassing moments

## A Sunday afternoon

1 What situations might make you feel *embarrassed*?

With another student, think of two or three situations. Here are some examples:
- After a meal in a restaurant, you realise you have no money with you.
- You see someone you've met before, and you can't remember their name.
- You forget a close friend's birthday.

Compare your ideas with other students. Have any of these things actually happened to you?

2 ▣ You will hear a woman telling a story about an embarrassing occasion. The story is in eight sections. Each time the tape stops, try to guess what will happen in the next section, and complete the sentences.

Section 2   Suddenly I heard . . .
Section 3   I opened the door, and I saw . . .
Section 4   They said . . .
Section 5   So I . . .
Section 6   When my husband came back . . .
Section 7   Then we discovered that . . .
Section 8   So they . . .

3 These pictures show elements in the story. What are they, and how do they fit into the story?

▣ Listen to the story again and check your answers.

# B Two stories

1 Look at the two pictures.
What do you think is happening in each picture?
What is just about to happen?

2   📼  You will hear the first part of two stories. Listen and answer the
questions.

*Story A*
Where was the speaker? Why was she there?
What time of year was it? What was the weather like?
What were other people doing?
What did the dogs do?

*Story B*
Where was the speaker? Why was he there?
Who did he see?
What did she look like?
What did he decide to do?

3 Make up an ending for each story. Write it down in one or two sentences.
Then show what you have written to another student.

4   📼  Listen to the complete stories. Why were these 'embarrassing moments'?
Give two reasons for each story:

Story A: Because the woman . . . and because . . .

Story B: Because the woman . . . and because . . .

# 4 | Conversations in public

## A Background noise

1 Imagine you are in these places:
- a railway station
- a busy street
- a restaurant

What sounds do you think you would hear? Make three lists of possible sounds, one for each place. Then compare your lists with another student's.

2 🔲 On the tape, you will hear background noises recorded in the three places. How many of the sounds in your lists can you hear? Are there any other sounds that are not in your lists?

3 🔲 You will hear three conversations with noise in the background. Listen and do the tasks below.

A 1 Fill the gaps in this sentence:

Trains leave at ................................. past the hour, and it takes ................................. to get to Sevenoaks.

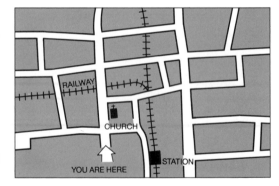

2 What does the woman decide to do?

B Mark the Commodore Hotel on the map.

C The conversation is between four people: Robert, Aisha, Tim and Mel. Choose the correct answers:

1 Robert introduces (a) Aisha (b) Mel to the others.
2 (a) Aisha (b) Mel has just arrived.
3 Aisha and Mel have met before because (a) they worked in the same place (b) they lived in the same place.
4 They are just about to (a) order a meal (b) start eating.

4 🔲 If necessary, listen to the conversations again without the background noise, and check your answers.

16

# B Opening lines

1 Imagine you are at a party and you want to start a conversation with someone you don't know. Think of other 'opening lines' like those in the picture. Write down as many as you can.

2 ▭ Listen to the six opening lines on the tape. Imagine that someone you don't know says them to *you* at a party. Which of the remarks seem to you:
   – friendly?
   – unfriendly?
   – too friendly?

Think of a suitable reply to each remark and write it down.

3 ▭ Now listen to the complete conversations and answer these questions:

   1 What does the woman want?
   2 What is special about the balcony?
   3 Where was (a) the man (b) the woman last Christmas?
   4 What is the man's occupation?
   5 Has the man worked in this department for long?
   6 Whose shirt is it?

Were any of the replies the same as those you wrote down?

4 Now try out your own 'opening lines' with other people in the class. Try to develop them into short conversations.

# 5 | Views

## A View over Athens

1    On the tape, a woman describes the view from her room in Athens. She mentions *four* of the views shown in the pictures. Put them in the order in which she describes them. Which views doesn't she mention?

   1 ...............    2 ...............    3 ...............    4 ...............

2    Listen to the tape again. Here are some words the woman uses, arranged in pairs. How are the words in each pair connected?

   her room – her parents' house        cars – colours
   the church – loudspeakers            morning – smog

3    **Extension**    Think of the view from your own house or flat. Write a list of things you can see. Show your list to another student and talk about the things you have written.

18

# B Views of Britain

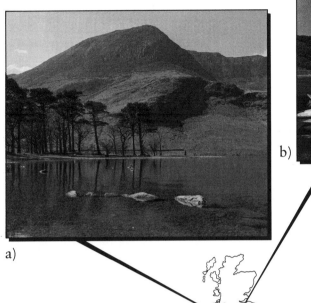

a)

b)

c)

1 Which of these views shows:
   a lake?
   an estuary?
   the sea?
   cliffs?
   mud flats?
   mountains?

2 ▭ You will hear nine sentences. Which of the views do you think each one describes? Could they describe more than one view? Listen and complete the table.

|   | Picture (a) | Picture (b) | Picture (c) |
|---|---|---|---|
| 1 |   |   |   |
| 2 |   |   |   |
| 3 |   |   |   |
| 4 |   |   |   |
| 5 |   |   |   |
| 6 |   |   |   |
| 7 |   |   |   |
| 8 |   |   |   |
| 9 |   |   |   |

3 ▭ You will hear three people describing the views. Listen and match them to the pictures.

4 Can you answer these questions?

1 Which way does the room face? What happens at low tide?
2 What's special about the house? What does the speaker enjoy doing?
3 Why does the speaker like the view? What's the weather like?

▭ Listen again and check your answers.

5 **Extension** Work with another student. Think of a 'favourite' view, or a view you know well. Describe it to your partner.

# 6 | On the line

## A Answerphone messages

1   🖭   You will hear seven messages that Jill Brown received on her telephone answering machine. Listen and make brief notes about each person and his/her message.

| Caller | Who are they? | Message |
|---|---|---|
| 1 Sue | Business partner | Forgot to cancel appointment. Ring John Gregson. |
| 2 Roger | | |
| 3 Whites | | |
| 4 Liz | | |
| 5 Steve | | |
| 6 Claire | | |
| 7 Roger | | |

2   🖭   Which of the messages does Jill Brown need to take action on? Imagine today is Monday. Listen again and complete this page from her diary.

| | |
|---|---|
| Monday | |
| Tuesday | |
| Wednesday | |
| Thursday | |
| Friday | |

3   From the messages, what can you tell about Jill Brown? Write down things you think you know about her (her work, her lifestyle, her friends, things she has done recently).

Now compare what you have written with another student.

# B Phone calls

1   ▱ You will hear someone called Anna talking on the telephone to five people. Write 1, 2, 3, 4 or 5 in the column.

Which person:
— met Anna at a party?   ............................
— is recovering from 'flu?   ........................
— wants to speak to Jimmy?   ........................
— has just returned from abroad?   ..............
— has just moved to the same
  town as Anna?   ...........................
— was planning to go
  swimming with Anna?   ...........................
— has just been on a car journey?   .................
— is meeting Anna the next day?   ...................
— is a complete stranger?   ...........................

2   ▱ Listen to each conversation again. Make notes in two lists:

— things you are sure about the other person
— things you are not sure about the other person

| | Sure | Not sure |
|---|---|---|
| 1 | Phone number: 663-2453 | Man or woman? |
| | | |
| | | |
| | | |
| | | |
| | | |
| | | |
| | | |

# 7 | Intruders

## A Scare stories

You will hear two people talking about times when they felt scared.

1   🔲 Listen to the beginning of each story. Imagine this happened to you. What would you do? Would you:
- hide?        – take no notice?
- run away?    – do something else?
- call for help?

2   How do you think the two stories continue? Which of these pictures do you think go with each one?

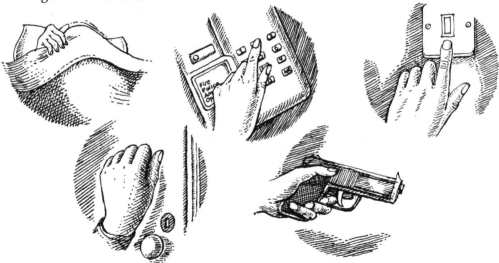

3   🔲 You will hear each story divided into sections. After each section, try to guess what will happen next.

4   **Extension**   Have any of these things happened to you (or have you ever been afraid they would happen)?
- Someone broke into your home.
- Someone threatened you with a gun or a knife.
- An animal attacked you.

Work with another student. Tell your partner about what happened.

# B Jigsaw story

1   📼   You will hear sentences from a story (not in their correct order). As you listen, try to piece the story together. Write short notes beside each question.

Where did this happen?

When did it happen?

What was the woman doing?

Why was the man there?

Were they friends or strangers?

Was the woman pleased to see him?

How did she feel?

What did she do?

What did the man do?

What did the neighbour do?

2   📼   Now listen to the whole story and complete the summary below.

A woman was alone in ................................................ when she heard

................................................ . Then she saw ................................................ .

So she ................................................, but the man

................................................ . In the end, the man

................................................, and the woman

................................................ . The neighbour

had thought ................................................ .

# 8 | Childhood

## A Buried treasure

On the tape, a woman remembers something that happened when she was four years old, when she and her sisters went to look for treasure.

1   Before you listen, look at the pictures. What do you think is happening in them? What do you think the story is?

2   📼 Listen to the tape. What do the pictures show? What happened between the pictures?

3   Here are some key words. How do they fit into the story?

   biscuits   a sledgehammer   a ploughed field   gold   leaves   a tree

4   📼 Now listen to the sentences from the tape and check your answers.

5   **Extension**   Did any of these things happen to you as a child?
   – You found something valuable.
   – You had a narrow escape.
   – You did something you couldn't tell your parents about.

Work with another student. Tell your partner your story, and find out what happened to him/her.

# B Party games

1 The pictures show what you need to play four different children's party games.

How do you think each game is played?

A

thimble

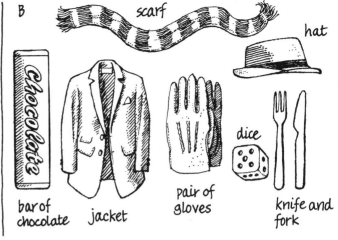

scarf

hat

bar of chocolate   jacket   pair of gloves   dice   knife and fork

C

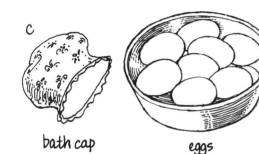

bath cap   eggs   towel

D

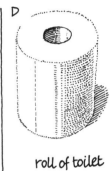

roll of toilet paper

2 🔲 You will hear children describing the four games. How are the things in the pictures used?

3 Which of the games do you think these sentences apply to?
🔲 Listen again and complete the table.

|  | Game |
|---|---|
| You all sit in a circle.<br>One person has to leave the room.<br>You choose a friend to play the game with.<br>You have to be as quick as you can.<br>You have to wait your turn.<br>The first person to finish is the winner.<br>You usually get in a terrible mess. | B, C |

4 **Extension**   Think of a party game you know. Tell your partner about it.
   – What do you need to play it?
   – How many people do you need?
   – How do you play it?
   – How do you win?

25

# 9 | Bought and sold

## A Morning market

1   Look at the things in the pictures here and on the opposite page. What are they called in English? (Use a dictionary to help you.)

Which of these things:
 – do you have yourself?
 – does someone you know have?

Which of the things would you most like to have? Why?

2   🔲 You will hear part of a radio programme called 'Morning Market'.
What is the purpose of the programme?
Which of the things in the pictures are the people selling?

3   🔲 Listen again and complete the table with as many details as you can.

|       |   | Item | Details | Price |
|-------|---|------|---------|-------|
| Sue   | 1 |      |         |       |
|       | 2 |      |         |       |
|       | 3 |      |         |       |
| Nick  | 1 |      |         |       |
|       | 2 |      |         |       |
|       | 3 |      |         |       |
| Julie |   |      |         |       |

4   **Extension**   Think of three things you'd like to sell and write them down.
Decide a price.
Form a group with other students and offer your items for sale. Give a few details about them.

# B What do you think of it?

1   🔲  You will hear five people talking about things they have just bought. What are they talking about? Match their conversations with the pictures. How can you tell?

2   Can you answer these questions?

1  Who is it for?
Why has he bought it?
How much did it cost?

2  Who is it for?
What will he use it for?
How much did it cost?

3  Who is it for?
What can you do with it?

4  Who is it for?
Where is he going?
What will he do with it?

5  Who is it for?
What will he do with it?
How do you make it work?

🔲  Now listen again and check your answers.

3   **Extension**   Choose one of the things in the pictures. Imagine:
– where you bought it
– how much it cost
– who it is for
– why you bought it

Tell another student about it, but do not name the object. See if he/she can guess what you have bought.

Now choose something else (not in the pictures), and repeat the activity.

# 10 | Behind the picture

## A Blackhouse

1 Look at the photograph and discuss these questions:
 1 How old do you think the photo is?
 2 Where do you think the picture was taken? In a hot or a cold country? In Europe? In a town or the country?
 3 What can you tell about the people? Are they rich or poor? Why is the woman carrying pots and buckets? What is her occupation? Do you think they live in the cottage?
 4 What can you tell about the house? What is it made of? Do you think it would be pleasant to live in?
 5 The kind of house shown in the picture was called a 'blackhouse'. Can you think of a reason for this name?

2 ▭ Listen to the tape. How does the woman answer these questions?

3 ▭ In the last part, the woman describes how she first saw the picture. Listen and complete the sentences.
 – A man found the photographs in . . .
 – He decided to go . . .
 – He visited the woman and . . .
 – He asked her if she knew . . .
 – When they went outside, they realised that . . .

# B The Scream

1 Look at the picture and discuss these questions:

1 Is it a picture of a man or a woman?

2 What does the picture show? A road? A bridge? Is it by the sea? By a river? By a lake?

3 What is the person doing? Running? Walking? Standing still?

4 Who are the people in the background? Do they know the person who is screaming?

5 Here are some explanations of the picture. Choose the one you think (a) is most likely (b) is most interesting.
   – The person is running away from the people in the distance.
   – The person is hiding, so that other people won't know he/she is screaming.
   – The person is screaming for help, but no one can hear him/her.
   – The person is screaming because something terrible has happened.

6 Which of these feelings does the picture seem to express?

| | |
|---|---|
| loneliness | fear |
| sadness | anger |
| despair | depression |
| beauty | happiness |

*'The Scream' by Edvard Munch, 1895*

2 ▭ You will hear someone talking about the picture. Listen to the first part. What answers does he give to the questions?

3 Look at the lines in the picture. Which are:

horizontal? 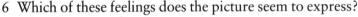  diagonal? 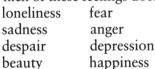  vertical?

▭ Listen to the last part of the tape. What effect does the speaker think the lines have?

4 Do you like this picture? Do you think it's a good picture? Why/Why not?

# 11 | Believe it or not

## A Macbeth

1 Write two lists: one of things that are supposed to bring *good luck* in your country, and one of things that are supposed to bring *bad luck*. Think of objects, animals, words, numbers and actions.

Show your list to your partner. Do you believe in any of these things?

2 🔲 You will hear a woman talking about a superstition that is common among actors in the theatre. Listen and answer these questions about the picture:

1 What has the man done wrong?
2 What should he have said?
3 He will now have to do certain things to 'break the spell'. Which of these does the speaker mention?
   – turn round three times    – swear
   – say 'Macbeth' backwards    – shrug his shoulders
   – say 'Sorry'    – leave the room
   – knock on the door    – leave the theatre

3 Look at these two scenes from Shakespeare's *Macbeth*. Imagine that the production is very unlucky. What do you think might go wrong?

*Act 5 Scene 1*
Sleepwalking scene

*Act 5 Scene 8*
Fight scene

4 🔲 Now listen to the second part of the tape. What actually happened once in each of these two scenes?

30

# B Palm reading

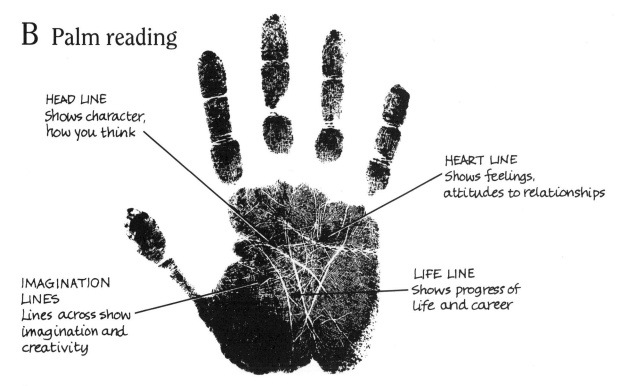

HEAD LINE
Shows character,
how you think

HEART LINE
Shows feelings,
attitudes to relationships

IMAGINATION
LINES
Lines across show
imagination and
creativity

LIFE LINE
Shows progress of
life and career

1 Here is the palm print of one of the authors of this book.
Compare it with your own hand. Can you find the same lines on your hand?
Do they look the same? Are they stronger, weaker, longer, shorter?
Do they have breaks in them? Do they branch into more than one line?

2 ⬛ Two people 'read' the author's palm.
Listen and mark in the table what each speaker says.

|  | Speaker 1 | Speaker 2 |
|---|---|---|
| He has a strong character. | | |
| He's unsure of himself. | | |
| When he was younger, he wasn't sure what to do. | | |
| He'll continue in the same job. | | |
| He'll have important relationships with two women. | | |
| He's a practical person. | | |
| He's an imaginative person. | | |
| He'll retire early. | | |

3 Compare the two palm readers. Is there anything they agree about? Do they
contradict each other at all?

4 **Extension** Work with another student. Look at your partner's palm and
find the lines shown in the illustration. Try reading your partner's palm.

31

# 12 | Bread and mushrooms

## A Making bread

1 The pictures show six stages in making bread. What does each picture show? Which sets of words do you think go with each picture?

Work with another student. Look at each set of words and discuss:

 – Which words can you actually see in the picture?
 – What do the other words mean? (Use a dictionary to help you.) How do you think they fit in the picture?

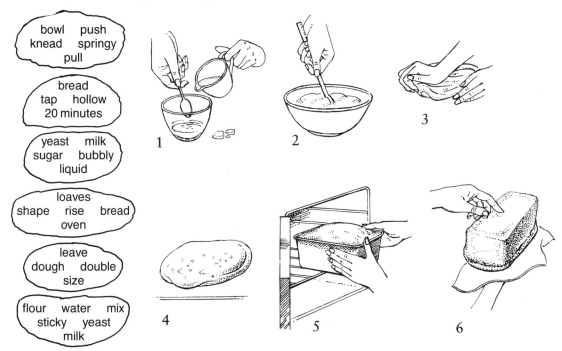

bowl    push
knead    springy
pull

bread
tap    hollow
20 minutes

yeast    milk
sugar    bubbly
liquid

loaves
shape    rise    bread
oven

leave
dough    double
size

flour    water    mix
sticky    yeast
milk

2 ▭ You will hear a man describing each stage. Listen and match the sets of words with the pictures.

3 Try to describe the stages yourself, using the words to make sentences.

4 **Extension** How is bread in your country different from the bread shown in the picture? Do you know how it is made?

32

# B Edible or poisonous?

1   Imagine you are very hungry and all you have to eat is the mushrooms in the picture. Which ones would you choose to eat?

2   ▭ You will hear someone describing the mushrooms. Listen and decide:

    1  Which are edible? Which are poisonous?
    2  Which of them is:
      – a field mushroom?
      – a fly agaric?
      – a cep?
      – a death cap?

3   ▭ Listen again and write the identifying features in the boxes.

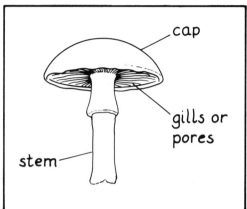

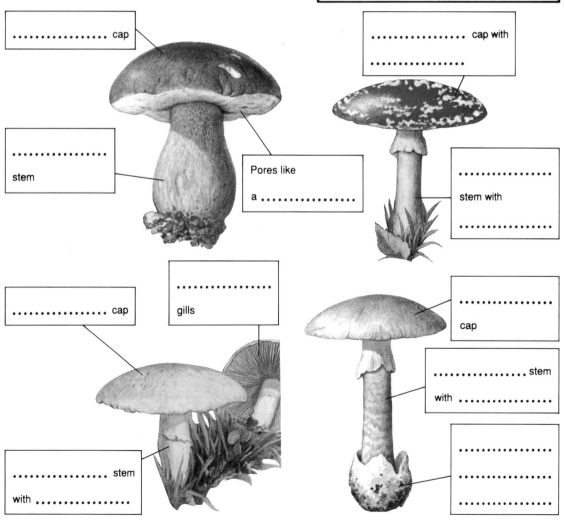

..................... cap

............... stem

Pores like a ...................

..................... cap with ...................

............... cap

stem with ...................

..................... cap

............... gills

............... stem with ...................

............... cap

............... stem with ...................

...................
...................
...................

33

# 13 | Learning to draw

## A The right side of your brain

1   Most people can't draw very well. Why do you think that is? And is there anything they can do about it?

Look at these opinions. Which do you agree with?
— Anybody can learn to draw well if they want to.
— Either you are naturally good at drawing or you're not. It isn't something you can learn.
— You can learn to draw by practice and by concentrating hard.
— To learn to draw, you must learn to use your brain in a different way.

2   ▭ On the tape, you will hear an artist saying how she thinks you can learn to draw.
Listen to the first part. Which of the opinions above does she seem to agree with? Which doesn't she agree with?

3   Your brain is in two halves: the left half is the practical side, and the right half is the imaginative side.

Which side do you think you use for:
speaking?                    dreaming?
making calculations?    reading?
appreciating beauty?    drawing?
keeping a sense of time?

▭ Listen to the second part of the tape and check your answers.

4   ▭ Listen to the last part of the tape. The artist talks about:
— young children
— 12-year-old children
— secondary school
— homework and mathematics

What is the connection between these things and the two sides of the brain?

### Left or right?

Which side of your brain is most developed? Do this quiz and find out.

1 When you were at school, did you prefer (a) arts subjects (b) science subjects?
2 Do you prefer sports which (a) you do alone (b) are team games?
3 Do you remember your dreams vividly (a) often (b) seldom or never?
4 When talking, do you use (a) many gestures (b) very few gestures?
5 Clasp your hands. Is your right thumb (a) on top (b) underneath?
6 When guessing the time, are your estimates (a) wrong by more than 10 minutes (b) accurate within 10 minutes?
7 Do you best remember (a) people's faces (b) their names?
8 With both eyes open, hold up a pencil in line with a window frame. Close your left eye, and notice how far the pencil moves. Now do the same with your right eye closed. Did the pencil move least with (a) the left eye shut (b) the right eye shut?

**Score** by adding the (a)s and (b)s. **More (a)s than (b)s** shows the right side of your brain is dominant. **More (b)s than (a)s** shows the left side of your brain is dominant.

# B A drawing exercise

1   You will do an exercise to help you use the right side of your brain.

Before you begin, look at these expressions and check that you understand what they mean:

| | |
|---|---|
| upside down | copy the drawing |
| turn it round | the spaces between the lines |
| the top of the drawing | a jigsaw puzzle |

2   Take a piece of paper and a pen or pencil.

    ▭ Listen, and follow the artist's instructions.

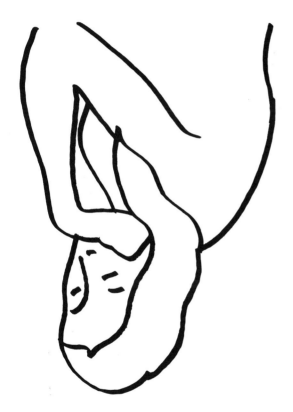

3   ▭ When you've finished, listen to the last part of the tape.

4   Show your drawing to the person next to you and say what you thought of the exercise. Do you think:
   – it helped you to learn to draw?
   – it helped you to see things differently?
   – it was interesting?

The ideas in Unit 13 are based on Betty Edwards' book *Drawing on the Right Side of the Brain* (Fontana/Collins).

# 14 | Male and female

## A Men and women

1 How different are men and women? And are the differences 'natural' or learnt?

Which of these statements do you agree with? Put a √, x or ?.

1 Men and women are exactly the same.
2 Men and women are mainly different because of their upbringing.
3 Men and women become different mainly because they have different roles in life.
4 The differences between men and women are natural and inborn.
5 Men are naturally better at certain things than women.
6 Women are naturally better at certain things than men.

Now compare your answers with another student.

2 ▭ You will hear someone talking about things she thinks women usually do better, and things she thinks men do better. Listen, and choose sentences from the table below.

| Men | are | better | at doing more than one thing at a time |
| Women | | worse | at reading maps |
| | | | at developing relationships |
| because | | they like to make things easy to understand. |
| | | they find it easier to talk about personal things. |
| | | they learn to please other people from an early age. |
| | | they don't like things to be too definite. |
| | | they're used to bringing up children. |

3 ▭ Listen again, and make brief notes on what the woman says about these topics:
  – men washing dishes
  – herself washing dishes
  – men and the universe
  – women's conversations
  – men's conversations
  – men and football

Do you agree with her?

# B Girls and boys

1    In the pictures, what games are the girls playing? What are the boys playing?
Do the pictures seem to you (a) quite normal? (b) rather unusual? Do you
think any pictures should be the other way round? If so, why?

2    🔲 You will hear three people talking about how boys and girls play.
According to them, which of these sentences are true of girls? Which are true
of boys?
- They run around more.
- They're more aggressive.
- They cooperate more.
- They play more with weapons.
- They take up more space.
- They're more peaceful.

3    🔲 You will hear the same people explaining what they think influences
girls and boys and makes them behave differently.

Listen and correct these three texts.

**A**   The teacher at the playgroup treats
the boys and the girls in exactly the
same way. If a girl is playing with a
train and a boy wants it, the teacher
tells the boy to wait his turn.

**B**   When they are very young, girls tend
to copy their mothers and boys copy
their fathers. Television also has a
strong influence on girls – they copy
the women they see on television, who
are often shown doing violent things.

**C**   When he was very young, my son used to play
typical boys' games. But when he went to nursery
school he started to play girls' games too. At the
same time he started watching television, but this
had no effect on him at all.

Which of the three explanations do you agree with yourself? Which do you
disagree with?

# 15 | Bees

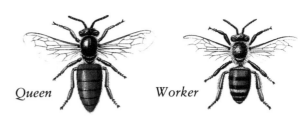

Queen          Worker

Drone

## A Life in the hive

1 How much do you know about bees?

Which of these sentences do you think are true, and which are false?
(Write T or F.)

1 The queen bee lays eggs.                                    ................
2 The workers collect nectar from flowers.                    ................
3 The queen bee turns the nectar into honey.                  ................
4 The workers look after the young bees in the hive.          ................
5 Drones are female bees.                                     ................
6 The drones' job is to guard the hive.                       ................
7 The drones die at the end of the summer.                    ................

Compare your answers with other students.

2 ▭ On the tape, you will hear a beekeeper talking about life in a beehive.

Listen and label the pictures. What kind of bees do they show? What are they doing?

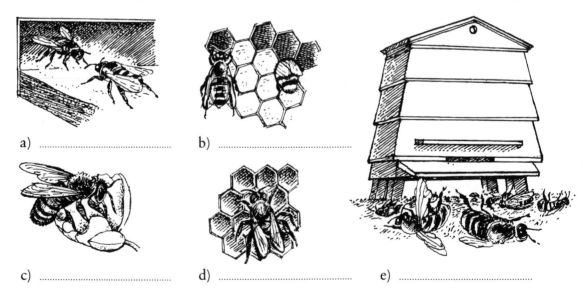

a) ..................................    b) ..................................    

c) ..................................    d) ..................................    e) ..................................

3 Now look at the sentences above again. Correct the false sentences so that all the
sentences are true. Can you add any more true sentences after listening to the tape?

# B Catching a swarm

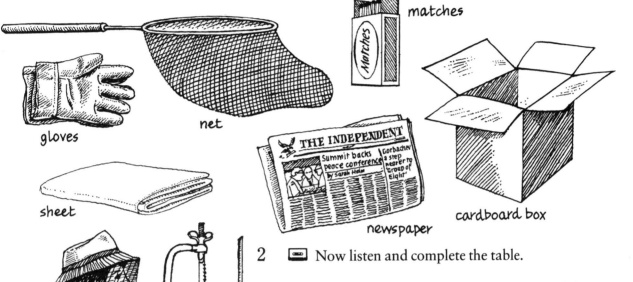

1   In this part, the beekeeper explains
    how to catch a swarm of bees and
    move it to a new hive.

    Before you listen, look at the objects below. Which ones do you think
    would be useful for catching a swarm of bees? Try to imagine how you
    would use them.

gloves

net

matches

cardboard box

sheet

newspaper

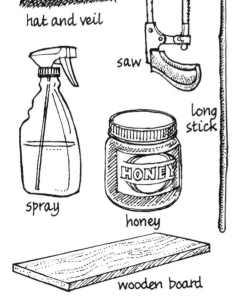

hat and veil

saw

long
stick

spray

honey

wooden board

2   📼 Now listen and complete the table.

| What you do | What for? |
| --- | --- |
| 1 Put on special clothes | So that the bees don't sting you |
| 2 | To keep the bees occupied |
| 3 | For the bees to fall into |
| 4 | To stop the bees escaping |
| 5 | So that the bees will feel at home |
| 6 | To help them get into the hive |

3   **Extension**   Using the notes you made in the
    table, write a short paragraph describing how to
    catch a swarm of bees. Begin, 'When you see a
    swarm of bees . . .'

# 16 | Emergency

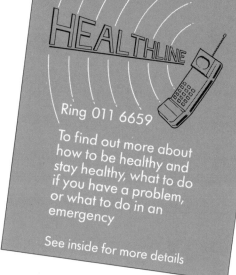

**HEALTHLINE**

Ring 011 6659

To find out more about how to be healthy and stay healthy, what to do if you have a problem, or what to do in an emergency

See inside for more details

## A Healthline

1    How much do you know about heart attacks? Choose the best answers to these questions.

1 Most heart attacks are caused by:
 - your heart beating too fast.
 - blood not reaching your heart.
 - your heart working too hard.
2 When you have a heart attack, you feel pain:
 - across your chest and into your arms.
 - all over the left side of your chest.
 - just where your heart is.

3 Heart attacks:
 - occur suddenly and without warning.
 - start slowly and gradually.
 - may be sudden or gradual.
4 Heart attacks:
 - never last more than a few minutes.
 - usually last for about 15 minutes.
 - can last for up to an hour.

2    📼 You will hear the first part of a telephone helpline which gives information about heart attacks. Listen and check your answers to the questions above.

3    The remarks below show what six people did when a friend had a heart attack. Do you think the people's actions were right or wrong? Put a ✓ or ✗.

*Right or wrong?*

1 'I called an ambulance, then I sat beside the patient and told her not to worry.'
2 'I lifted the patient up carefully and put her in the back of the car, then drove her to hospital.'
3 'I lay the patient on her back on the floor and put a pillow under her head.'
4 'I gave the patient a glass of cold water.'
5 'I undid the buttons of his shirt and put a blanket round him.'
6 'He stopped breathing, so I breathed into his mouth and pushed my hand down on his chest.'

📼 Now listen to the second part of the recording and check your answers.

4    📼 Listen to the second part of the recording again and write down five things you should do if someone has a heart attack.

# B Street incident

1 Imagine you see one of these incidents:
   - two youths attack an old woman and steal her handbag
   - a pickpocket steals a wallet from a man's jacket
   - a man shoots a young woman and then runs away
   - a middle-aged man collapses just in front of you
   - a dog attacks a small boy and bites his arm

   What would you do? Help? Get other people to help? Or do nothing?
   Compare your ideas with other students.

2   ▭ You will hear a man describe an incident he saw in the street. You will
   hear the story in four sections. After each section, stop and answer the
   questions.

   *Section 1*
   Where was the man? What was he doing?
   What did he hear? What do you think the noise was?
   What do you think he did next?

   *Section 2*
   What did the man do?
   What was wrong with the woman?
   He saw someone running away. Who do you think it was?
   What do you think the man should do now?

   *Section 3*
   What did the man do?
   Why do you think people ignored the woman?
   What do you think will happen next?

   *Section 4*
   Who was the man in the car?
   What did he do?
   What do you think happened after that? Imagine an ending for the story.

3   **Extension**   Work with another student.
   Student A: You are a police officer investigating the incident. Ask student B
   what he/she saw.
   Student B: Imagine you saw this incident from the other side of the street.
   Answer the police officer's questions.

# 17 | Punishing children

## A Smacking

### Report reveals parents' guilt

NINE out of ten parents smack their children but half feel guilty about it according to a survey out

1   Look at the newspaper headline.
What do you think the report might say about punishing children?

🎧 You will hear an interview with a woman from *Children* magazine. Which of the things below does the report say? Listen and mark each statement 'Yes' or 'No'.

1  Most parents in Britain smack their children.          ................

2  Very few parents smack their children every day.          ................

3  Many parents fail to see things from the child's point of view.          ................

4  If children misbehave, they have to be punished.          ................

5  Children are often naughty because they want more love.          ................

2   🎧 You will hear four people say what they think about punishing children. Listen and match them with the opinions below.

**A** It's no good trying to explain things to very young children. Smacking is more honest and quicker than other forms of punishment.

**B** If you're violent towards children, it teaches them to be violent. It's better to try to talk to them.

**C** A quick smack doesn't do children any harm, and it works.

**D** Instead of punishing them, you can tell children what they've done wrong. If you punish children, they'll always remember it and hate you for it.

3   Discuss these questions:

– Which speaker's views are most similar to your own?
– How old do you think each of the speakers is?
– In your own country, do older people have different ideas about punishing children from younger people? How are they different?

# B Zen and the art of punishment

1 Look at the picture.
What is the child doing?

Imagine doing this as a punishment
for behaving badly. Does it seem to
you to be:
— a good form of punishment?
— a strange form of punishment?
— a ridiculous form of punishment?
Why?

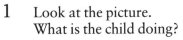 You will hear a woman talking about a Chinese friend.
Listen to the first part of the tape and complete these sentences:

— Her friend's father was a . . .
— As a punishment in his family, the children had to . . .

2 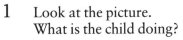 Listen to the second part of the
tape and find five things wrong or
missing in this description:

> 'Well, it's quite easy really. You just get some
> ink, dip your brush in it, and then make a few
> strokes on a piece of paper. Once you've got
> used to it, you can usually get it exactly right
> straight away, so you can do it very quickly
> without really thinking.'

3 Why would this be a good
punishment?
— because it's very boring to do
— because it's very frustrating to do
— because it makes you feel peaceful
— because it improves your mind
— because it makes you forget what
you did wrong
— any other reasons?

 Listen to the last part of the tape
and choose the best answers. Do you
agree with the speaker?

# 18 | Planet Earth

## A Traffic

1 Traffic congestion in towns causes delays and pollution.
Here are some possible solutions to the problem. Which do you think are
good solutions? Mark ✓, ✗ or ? in Column A.

|  | A | B |
|---|---|---|
| 1 Improve roads so that traffic moves faster. | | |
| 2 Make roads in cities narrower to discourage drivers. | | |
| 3 Limit parking places in towns. | | |
| 4 Make drivers pay more to use roads. | | |
| 5 Spend more money on improving public transport. | | |
| 6 Ban private cars from city centres. | | |
| 7 Set up a system of 'shared' taxis. | | |

2 ▭ You will hear part of a radio phone-in programme in which a
government minister, Mrs Fielding, answers questions from two callers.
Which of the opinions above does each caller express? In Column B, mark:
  1( = Frederick Bowles, the first caller) or
  2( = Joanna Briggs, the second caller).
Which solution is favoured by the government?

3 ▭ Here are three ideas expressed in the programme. According to Mrs
Fielding, what are the arguments against them? Listen again and make notes
in the table. Then compare what you have written with another student.

| Idea | Argument against |
|---|---|
| Spend more on public transport | |
| Make drivers pay more | |
| Discourage people from using cars in cities | |

4 **Extension** Discuss these questions with another student:
  – Is traffic congestion a problem in your own country? Where is it worst?
  – What is the government doing, and how successful are they?

# B Inside the greenhouse

1 Which of these commonly affect
your country?
   – droughts       – high temperatures
   – high winds     – low temperatures
   – heavy rain     – blizzards
   – floods         – sandstorms

Have any of them become more
frequent in recent years?

2 How would you answer these
questions?
   – Is the earth really getting warmer?
   – If so, are there any signs of it?

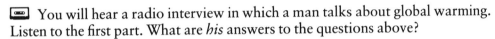 You will hear a radio interview in which a man talks about global warming.
Listen to the first part. What are *his* answers to the questions above?

Listen again and complete these sentences:
– Most scientists believe . . .
– In the last 10 years . . .
– In the next 100 years . . .

3 In the second part of the interview, the man talks about the effects of global
warming. What do you expect him to say about the topics in the table?

| | |
|---|---|
| The sea | |
| Coastal areas | |
| The USA and Russia | |
| The Mediterranean | |
| Food | |

Listen and see if you were right. Then use the table to make notes
about what he says.

4 **Extension**   What do you think will happen to the world's climate? Which
of these opinions do you agree with?
   – The world's climate has always changed. There's nothing special to worry
     about now. In some places, the change might even be for the better.
   – The Earth's climate is changing, but only very slowly. We'll be able to
     adapt to the changes.
   – Very soon, science will find a solution to the problem of global warming.
     Perhaps we will discover a way of reversing the process.
   – In a few decades, life as we know it will become impossible. It's already
     too late to do anything about it.

# 19 | Sporting moments

## A White water rafting

**1** How much do you think you would enjoy white water rafting? Would you find the experience:

    exciting?   frightening?   relaxing?

Try to imagine you have just been white water rafting. Write three sentences about the experience.

*Example:*

It was really exciting.
I got very cold and wet.
I fell in the water.

**2** 🔲 You will hear a woman talking about white water rafting in Costa Rica. Listen and decide which sentences are true (T) and which are false (F).

1 The river was fast and looked dangerous. .................
2 There were two people in each raft. .................
3 There were trees overhanging the river. .................
4 The guide told the speaker to put her head down. .................
5 She wasn't wearing a helmet. .................
6 Her head hit the branch of a tree. .................
7 She was knocked unconscious. .................
8 She enjoyed white water rafting. .................

**3** 🔲 Here are some words the speaker uses.
Listen to the tape again and match the adjectives with the nouns.

| *Adjectives* | *Nouns* |
|---|---|
| beautiful | (water)fall |
| fierce | rocks |
| cruel-looking | pool |
| rubber | feeling |
| quiet | water |
| huge | rafts |
| foaming | forests |
| exhilarating | river |

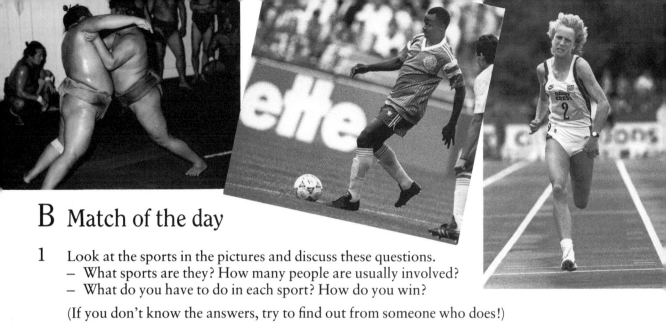

# B  Match of the day

1   Look at the sports in the pictures and discuss these questions.
    – What sports are they? How many people are usually involved?
    – What do you have to do in each sport? How do you win?

(If you don't know the answers, try to find out from someone who does!)

2   ▭  You will hear three sports commentaries.
    Match them with the sports in the pictures.

3   These people are mentioned in the commentaries:
    Fujino shin     Roger Milla     Kostic     Glenda Walsh
    Anne Murray        Onokuni        Higuita

    Which sports do they go with? What countries do they come from?

4   ▭  Listen to the commentaries again and complete these sentences.

    1  Onokuni, also known as ......................................................, is fighting against Fujino
       shin, whose nickname is ....................................................... Fujino shin weighs
       ...................................................., but Onokuni is ..................................................... heavier.
       .................................................... wins the fight, because he manages to
       .....................................................

    2  The match is being played in ...................................................... The two teams are
       .................................................... and .................................................... Higuita
       .................................................... to try to get the ball, but this allows
       .................................................... to ..................................................... So the score is
       ...................................................., and .................................................... are almost certain to
       win. This means they will play in the .....................................................

    3  With 80 metres to go, Glenda Walsh is ...................................................... But
       .................................................... overtakes her and ..................................................... Her
       time is ...................................................., which is a good win because it's only
       .................................................... this summer.

# 20 | War zones

## A Arrival in Beirut

1 Think of an airport in your own country. Imagine you've just arrived there by plane. Try to imagine the scene:
   a) from the plane window as you land
   b) as you step out of the plane
   c) as you enter the arrivals lounge

Write a list of things you 'see' in each scene. Then compare your list with another student.

a)　　　　　　　　　　　b)　　　　　　　　　　　c)

2 ▭ You will hear a woman remembering what it was like to arrive at Beirut Airport in the late 1970s. Listen and note down what she saw:
   a) from the plane
   b) as she stepped out of the plane
   c) in the arrivals lounge

3 The woman talks about people in the arrivals lounge. This diagram shows some of the things she says about them:

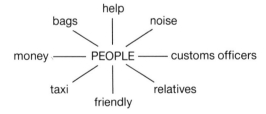

▭ Listen again. Then in your own words say how the words are connected.

# B Northern Ireland

1 Imagine you see a newspaper article about Northern Ireland. Which of these two pictures is the newspaper more likely to show? Why?

Which of these words do you associate with the idea of Northern Ireland?

soldiers    violence    normal    terror    beauty    tragedy

2 ▭ You will hear a woman talking about life in Northern Ireland. Which of the things below does she say? Listen and mark them with a ✓.

1 People find it impossible to carry on with their everyday lives. ................
2 The only obvious sign of anything unusual is the number of soldiers. ................
3 Things look normal on the surface, but in fact the fighting has changed people's lives. ................
4 Ordinary people have no reason to be afraid. ................
5 People try to pretend that everything is normal. ................
6 TV and newspapers give a false picture of life in Northern Ireland. ................
7 Most people from other countries are afraid to go there. ................
8 Northern Ireland would be a dangerous place to visit as a tourist. ................

3 ▭ You will hear sentences from the tape. Listen and check your answers again.

4 **Extension** All round the world there are places like Lebanon and Northern Ireland where fighting continues without any solution. Do you think there is anything that (a) individuals, (b) governments, (c) the United Nations can do to help?

# Tapescript

## Unit 1   Music in the mind

### 1A   Mental images

#### EXERCISE 1

*Excerpt from a piece of flute and koto music*

#### EXERCISE 2

1  It makes me think of moonlight on the Taj Mahal, and elephants – somewhere hot and steamy and far away in the moonlight.

2  I can, I think I can picture a tent, and I think particularly the inside of a . . . a kind of Arabian tent and er I can also see very much um a fan, maybe, maybe kind of er somebody waving a fan, keeping us all cool, and there would be um – it's the end of a marvellous oriental type of banquet, and we're all relaxing and enjoying ourselves.

3  This music definitely makes me think of the outside, high up, possibly travelling on a horse, the mountains, the night coming on, a slight chill in the air, um animals in the distance.

4  It makes me think of a very, a very big landscape, very cold, very empty. I don't know whether it's a mountain, I don't know whether it's a great plain but it's, it's empty and there is something in it, perhaps I'm there, I don't know, but I feel alone, I feel lonely and I feel hopeless.

5  I find that reminds me of a rather cosy sort of garden, but a very peaceful place where there's maybe waterfalls and a stream going through and very nice arrangements of flowers everywhere.

### 1B   Musical memories

#### EXERCISE 1

1  *Excerpt from Beethoven's 4th Piano Concerto*

I think this piece of music has importance to me because I think it was the first time that I'd ever been in a big concert hall, the Albert Hall in London. And hearing music in the place it's meant to be played, in a concert hall as against a record, makes a big impact on you.

2  *Excerpt from James Taylor's 'First of May'*

Well, it's called 'First Day of May' and it's about spring breaking, and it reminds me of my home in Athens, Georgia, um at the University of Georgia during spring, which is one of the most wonderful times of the year there.

#### EXERCISE 2

1  I think this piece of music has importance to me because I think it was the first time that I'd ever been in a big concert hall, the Albert Hall in London. And hearing music in the place it's meant to be played, in a concert hall as against a record, makes a big impact on you. It was also the first time I'd really heard what they call a 'serious' piece of music, as opposed to 'pop' music. And I also remember it because it was a very balmy, gentle, warm, summer night in London. And I didn't go into the bottom of the Albert Hall, I went to the very top, the very top gallery, where there are no seats, so you wander round. And what surprised me was, it was er it wasn't just an audience of students. There were men from the City in suits and bowler hats lying on the floor, some of them with newspapers over their faces so they could concentrate on the music better. There were people holding

hands, people throwing paper aeroplanes over the top, and it was like being in the middle of a market place, except there was this lovely music drifting up, and it was Beethoven's 4th Piano Concerto. It was the first time I'd heard it, and it's a beautiful piece of music.

2 Well, it's called 'First Day of May' and it's about spring breaking, and it reminds me of my home in Athens, Georgia, um at the University of Georgia during spring, which is one of the most wonderful times of the year there. And when I hear that music I can see my old street that I lived on, and people throwing footballs in the yard, and the public swimming pool with all the students going there, and everyone walking around in shorts, and the sky being very blue. There's lots of festivals in the streets and a general good attitude is flowing through everything, it seems.

# Unit 2    Strangers in the street

## 2A    Excuse me . . .

### EXERCISE 2

1 Excuse me, love, would you like to buy a watch?
2 Excuse me, miss, can you help me, please. I need some money for the bus fare home.
3 Excuse me, sir, I'm collecting for International Aid. Can you spare some money?
4 Excuse me, madam, I wonder if you could spare me just five minutes of your time. I'm doing some market research for a fast food company. I wonder if you could possibly manage to just answer five simple questions.

### EXERCISE 3

1 A: Excuse me, love, would you like to buy a watch?
  B: Er, no, no, thank you.

2 A: Excuse me, miss, can you help me, please. I need some money for the bus fare home.
  B: For the bus fare home? *(Yes.)* Well, how much do you need?

3 A: Excuse me, sir, I'm collecting for International Aid. Can you spare some money?
  B: Um, what's International Aid?

4 A: Excuse me, madam, I wonder if you could spare me just five minutes of your time. I'm doing some market research for a fast food company. I wonder if you could possibly manage to just answer five simple questions.
  B: Well, is it genuine market research or are you going to sell me something?

### EXERCISE 4

1 A: Excuse me, love, would you like to buy a watch?
  B: Er, no, no, thank you.
  A: Come on, they're only £9.99.
  B: No, really, no, honestly.
  A: Honestly, love, these are from Switzerland. They cost you £25 in the shops, I promise you.
  B: Yeah, but look I've got a perfectly good one . . .
  A: I tell you what, I tell you what, I tell you what, because it's a nice day, eight quid, eight pounds *(No, really.)* for a watch.
  B: No, thank you. I've got one, it works beautifully, I must go. Bye.
  A: Thank you.

2 A: Excuse me, miss, can you help me, please. I need some money for the bus fare home.
  B: For the bus fare home? *(Yes.)* Well, how much do you need?
  A: Er, would a pound be all right?
  B: Oh, goodness. I'm sorry, I haven't got a pound. Um, I can give you 20 pence.
  A: Oh, 20 pence isn't enough for my bus fare.
  B: I know, but that's all I've got. I've got to get home myself. I'm ever so sorry – I'd help you if I could.
  A: Oh, all right. Thank you very much.
  B: Good luck. Try someone else.

3 A: Excuse me, sir, I'm collecting for International Aid. Can you spare some money?
  B: Um, what's International Aid?
  A: It's um an organisation to help starving children in Africa, in various countries in Africa, not just one country.
  B: Ah, I see. Have you got any form of identification?
  A: Yes, here's my card.
  B: Ah. Well yes, yes, all right, I'll see what I've got.
  A: Thank you very much. Oh, thank you, sir – that's very kind.
  B: You're welcome.

4 A: Excuse me, madam, I wonder if you could spare me just five minutes of your time. I'm doing some market research for a fast food company. I wonder if you could possibly manage to just answer five simple questions.

B: Well, is it genuine market research or are you going to sell me something?

A: No, I'm not going to sell you something. Five simple questions.

B: Five minutes.

A: Oh, that's smashing. Um firstly, do you often use fast food outlets . . .

## 2B Fast food survey

### EXERCISE 2

A: Excuse me, do you mind answering a few questions?

B: No.

A: Um firstly, do you ever eat fast food?

B: Yes, yes, I do.

A: What kind of fast food do you normally eat?

B: Oh, er you know, burgers, sandwiches, well sometimes like a pizza or, you know, kebabs.

A: Oh, right. And how often do you eat fast food? Every day, more than once a week or less than once a week?

B: Er, well Monday to Friday when I'm working er, yeah every day, um but not not usually at the weekends.

A: And what time of day do you eat fast food?

B: Well, at work as I said, you know at lunchtime, um you know sort of go out and get a burger or a sandwich. Sometimes, you know, if if I'm going out and I've no time to cook in the evenings then I'll, I'll send out for a pizza.

A: Oh, right. Do you only eat it as a main meal or do you snack between meals?

B: No, only as a main meal, you know lunch or, or in the evening.

A: And what do you think of fast food? Which statements do you think are true? Um, either 'It's convenient'?

B: Oh, definitely. I mean, that's sort of the main reason that I eat it.

A: Right. How about 'It tastes good'?

B: Yeah. Um, I mean, not as good as food like in a, in a good restaurant, but it's not bad.

A: 'It's good for you'?

B: No. Sort of eating quickly and standing up it's sort of bad for you. The food itself isn't very good for you, you know there's not enough greens, um you know vegetables or salad.

A: Mm. How about 'It's an expensive way of eating'? What do you think of that?

B: Oh, yes, it is, er but you're paying for the convenience, you know the speed of it. Er, well, I certainly think that it's cheaper than you know cooking your own food.

A: Er, and what about lastly 'It creates litter'. Do you think that's true?

B: Yes, yes, it does. Only I, I always put mine in a you know in a litter bin, but er unfortunately a lot of people don't, um but in the packaging there is a lot of paper involved and plastic and sometimes polystyrene.

# Unit 3   Embarrassing moments

## 3A   Sunday afternoon

### EXERCISE 2

*Section 1*
It was a quiet, sunny and very sleepy Sunday afternoon and I was sitting out in the garden reading the Sunday newspapers, not expecting anything at all, the children were out playing, and thinking that I had a couple of hours of peace and quiet.

*Section 2*
And I heard a large vehicle arriving at the end of the garden, and then I heard a loud knocking on the door, in the front of the house.

*Section 3*
And I went out, and there were about twelve, um elderly ladies wearing their Sunday best clothes, er hats and white cardigans and carrying their handbags, looking very happy and very friendly.

*Section 4*
And they said um, 'Well, we're sorry, we hope we're not late, but we couldn't find the house very easily', and obviously thought that this was the right place to be. And then one of them said very helpfully, 'Well your husband was very kind in inviting us to tea'. So I thought, 'Good gracious, my husband must have gone mad or forgotten to tell me'.

*Section 5*
So I asked them into the house, and they started taking off their, one or two took off their coats and they sat down and they started chatting quite happily. And they asked me about my

children, and I did have children, and they talked about how beautiful the village was, and it was indeed very beautiful.

*Section 6*
Then when my husband appeared they didn't speak to him, and I thought this was surprising because they said that they were, they'd been invited by him. And he looked a bit shocked to see them all sitting there.

*Section 7*
And then er we quickly discovered that it was the wrong husband and the wrong house and they were in fact expected at a house on the other side of the village.

*Section 8*
So they were very embarrassed and red-faced and said how sorry they were, and I was very pleased that they were in the wrong house, and they went walking down through the village to the right house.

## EXERCISE 3

It was a quiet, sunny and very sleepy Sunday afternoon and I was sitting out in the garden reading the Sunday newspapers, not expecting anything at all, the children were out playing, and thinking that I had a couple of hours of peace and quiet. And I heard a large vehicle arriving at the end of the garden, and then I heard a loud knocking on the door, in the front of the house. And I went out, and there were about twelve, um elderly ladies wearing their Sunday best clothes, er hats and white cardigans and carrying their handbags, looking very happy and very friendly. And they said um, 'Well, we're sorry, we hope we're not late, but we couldn't find the house very easily', and obviously thought that this was the right place to be. And then one of them said very helpfully, 'Well your husband was very kind in inviting us to tea'. So I thought, 'Good gracious, my husband must have gone mad or forgotten to tell me'. So I asked them into the house, and they started taking off their, one or two took off their coats and they sat down and they started chatting quite happily. And they asked me about my children, and I did have children, and they talked about how beautiful the village was, and it was indeed very beautiful. Then when my husband appeared they didn't speak to him, and I thought this was surprising because they said that they were, they'd been invited by him. And he looked a bit shocked to see them all sitting there. And then er we quickly discovered

that it was the wrong husband and the wrong house and they were in fact expected at a house on the other side of the village. So they were very embarrassed and red-faced and said how sorry they were, and I was very pleased that they were in the wrong house, and they went walking down through the village to the right house.

## 3B   Two stories

### EXERCISE 2

*Story A*
Well, a couple of years ago we had a very hot summer, and every day I used to take my dog for a walk. Because it was a hot day the park was full of people all reading, half asleep, having a lovely time, listening to their radios, and I was walking my dog. And suddenly I saw another big black dog appear, and it ran towards my dog, and the two got into a fight.

*Story B*
It was some years ago and it was in a supermarket. And I was doing some shopping there, and I suddenly saw a young person, or I thought I saw a young person that I knew. She had her back to me, and she was rather short and she had long blonde hair. And I thought it would be rather funny if I gave her a surprise. So I crept up behind her and I just tugged her hair, gave her hair a little pull.

### EXERCISE 4

*Story A*
Well, a couple of years ago we had a very hot summer, and every day I used to take my dog for a walk. Because it was a hot day the park was full of people all reading, half asleep, having a lovely time, listening to their radios, and I was walking my dog. And suddenly I saw another big black dog appear, and it ran towards my dog, and the two got into a fight. I ran towards the dogs to try and, to to break them up, and as I got hold of one of the dogs the other dog bit my skirt. So they actually pulled my skirt off, and I was left in my knickers with the two dogs running away with my skirt, and I had a park full of people watching me while I ran acro- ran right across and tried to catch my skirt. It was a very very embarrassing moment.

*Story B*
It was some years ago and it was in a supermarket. And I was doing some shopping there, and I suddenly saw a young person, or I

thought I saw a young person that I knew. She had her back to me, and she was rather short and she had long blonde hair. And I thought it would be rather funny if I gave her a surprise. So I crept up behind her and I just tugged her hair, gave her hair a little pull. And to my, well, horror really, the hair came off, and the woman that turned round was middle-aged and she'd been wearing false hair, and she was not very pleased at my joke.

# Unit 4 Conversations in public

## 4A Background noise

### EXERCISE 2

*Series of background noises:*
1 *Railway station*
2 *Street*
3 *Restaurant*

### EXERCISE 3

**A** – Excuse me, can you tell me if I can get direct to Sevenoaks from here?
   – Sevenoaks? Yes, well, it would be a stopping train, but you can actually go to Sevenoaks – the trains go at 32 minutes past the hour, (*Yes.*) but that would be a stopping train.
   – Stopping, you mean it's a slow one?
   – It stops at every station.
   – Right, and how long's that journey?
   – That will take about, ooh one hour 20 minutes.
   – Oh, dear. OK, I'll have to do that then. Thank you. (*Right, fine.*)

**B** – Excuse me, (*Yeah.*) er I'm afraid I'm lost – I'm looking for the Commodore Hotel.
   – The Commodore? Oh yeah, the Commodore. Um, right, if you go straight down this road, er you then come to a church. Now you turn right at the church, and then you go over a, um over a railway bridge (*Railway bridge.*) yep. Carry, carry on till you get to the main road – you can't miss it, there's traffic lights there. Turn left and er it's it's just down down on your left.
   – It's quite some way, isn't it?
   – Yeah, it is a bit.
   – So it's right at the church. (*Yeah, that's right, yeah.*) And then I turn left when I get to the main road.

– Yeah, but you got to, once you, er yeah, over the railway bridge, turn left, and then it's on your left.
– Fine. OK, thank you very much.
– OK, you're welcome.

**C** – (*Hello.*) Ah, here she is. (*Hi.*) Aisha, how are you? (*Sorry I'm late.*) What, did you lose the, lose the way? (*Yes, I'm ever so sorry.*) Now who do you, you don't, do you know – Tim, this is Aisha, Tim, Tim who works with me in the office, (*Nice to meet you, hello.*) and Mel, who's, who's his girlfriend. (*Mel.*) (*Hello.*)
– We have met.
– We have, haven't we? (*Yes.*) Where did we meet?
– Goodness. Parties? Office? (*No.*) (*Small world!*) Where do you live?
– I just recognise your face.
– Were you at school together?
– Oh, I doubt it, no. (*No, no.*) Where do you live?
– Richmond.
– Oh, I used to live in Richmond.
– This is why. This is why. How nice to see you. (*And you!*) (*Well.*)
– Have you ordered? No. We were waiting for you to arrive, we thought . . .
– Oh, right. Can I have the menu?
– Yeah, sure.

### EXERCISE 4

(*Conversations from Exercise 3 repeated with no background noise.*)

## 4B Opening lines

### EXERCISE 2

1 Er, excuse me, I was um just wondering, I'm just popping up to the buffet to get a coffee, wondered if you, if you'd like me to get you anything.
2 It's lovely here, isn't it? Have you, have you been here before?
3 How lovely to see you again. Do you remember?
4 Excuse me, but I've just got to say this. You know, you have got the most extraordinary eyes.
5 Um, have you been working here for very long?
6 Excuse me, can I just ask you where you bought your shirt?

## EXERCISE 3

1  A: Er, excuse me, I was um just wondering, I'm just popping up to the buffet to get a coffee, wondered if you, if you'd like me to get you anything.
   B: Oh, that's very kind.
   A: What would you like?
   B: Oh yes, um, white please, no sugar.
   A: OK.

2  A: It's lovely here, isn't it? Have you, have you been here before?
   B: Oh yes I, I often come.
   A: Do you? (*Yes.*) It's a marvellous view from the balcony.
   B: Oh, oh you've been up there, have you? (*Yes.*) Oh, not a lot of people know that the balcony's there, but it's it's great once you see it.

3  A: How lovely to see you again. Do you remember?
   B: Um.
   A: Last Christmas.
   B: Uh, no.
   A: We were at the same party. That one in the country. With the log fires and the . . . (*No.*) You don't remember me?
   B: I was in London at Christmas.

4  A: Excuse me, but I've just got to say this. You know, you have got the most extraordinary eyes.
   B: How very kind.
   A: No, no, it's just you see, I'm an optician, (*Oh.*) and um eyes fascinate me, and you have got the most extraordinary eyes.

5  A: Um, have you been working here for very long?
   B: Oh yes, ages. (*Have you?*) Too long, some people say.
   A: I'm just surprised I haven't seen you before.
   B: I haven't been in this department very long.
   A: I see, so where were you before?
   B: On the fourth floor.

6  A: Excuse me, can I just ask you where you bought your shirt?
   B: Oh, actually funnily enough I didn't buy it. It actually belongs to a friend of mine. He left it at my house, and I haven't told him yet.
   A: It's just that I think it's absolutely wonderful.
   B: Oh, thanks.

# Unit 5   Views

## 5A   *View over Athens*

### EXERCISES 1 and 2

This room is on the top of a four-storey building. The building isn't particularly beautiful, nor is the room, but it's on, it has a very good view. It's on the top – it's, it's like a guest house almost on the top of my parents' house, and because it's quite high up I can see almost all of Athens.

Immediately opposite the room I can see a church, which is very nice – which can also be very annoying, because every Sunday morning they put loudspeakers in the, in the yard of the church and you can hear the whole service whether you want to or not.

And um beyond the church I can see the sea and the harbour, and that's the harbour of Piraeus. On the other side I can see the Acropolis and Lekavitos, which is a mountain in Athens with a church on the top as well.

It's very nice at night, because the whole city's lit up, and it looks beautiful, and you can see the different colours of the lights and you can see the cars forming colours in the streets as they drive by, etcetera, forming colours with their lights, I mean you know.

Um, sometimes it's not so nice, though, especially early in the morning when there's a lot of smog over the city, and you wake up to a smog cloud that covers everything. And the change is drastic, because on a clear day the view is so marvellous and so beautiful and the colours are so bright, and then on a day that's polluted with the smog the change is just . . . and you can't even breathe.

## 5B   *Views of Britain*

### EXERCISE 2

1  The setting sun is reflected with a hundred different shades of colour in the mud.

2  The view from my bedroom window looks out over a lake.

3  If you look out of the window you can see the river flowing by.

4  There's a line as far as the eye can see of rolling cliffs and little beaches.

5  The effect is magical because the view changes all the time with the weather.

6  It's one of the most peaceful places you could imagine.

7 One of the most attractive features of the view from the window is in the evening.

8 When the sun comes out the lake is just like a sheet of glass.

9 It's a very ordinary house, but the view is spectacular, it's very, very beautiful.

### EXERCISES 3 and 4

1 Well, the the house is alongside and overlooking the River Almond, which flows into the estuary of the Firth of Forth, and if you look out of the window you can see the river flowing by, quietly at low tide and quite quickly at high tide or when the um the weather changes. One of the most attractive features of the view from the window is in the evening because um it's a western vista, and the sun sets across the other side of the Firth of Forth, and when the tide is low and all the mud flats are disclosed, the setting sun is reflected with um a hundred different shades of colour in the mud, and it makes a marvellous panorama.

2 This room is in a house in Cornwall, which is in the south west of England – it's a very ordinary room, it's a very ordinary house, but the, the view is spectacular, it's very very beautiful. To start with you're looking at the sea, which is always nice, but on the, on the far side of this – I suppose you'd call it a harbour mouth – there's a line as far as the eye can see of rolling cliffs and little beaches, and the tide coming in. On nice days it's all very calm, on horrible days it crashes up the cliffside. It's often very wet, the rain lashes down, it's often very misty. And it's one of the most peaceful places you could imagine. You sit there in your chair and look out of the window, and time stands still.

3 The view from my bedroom window looks out over a lake, er and in the background is a range of quite, quite tiny mountains, but the effect is magical because the view changes all the time with, with the weather. This part of the country does tend to be a little bit wet, but when the sun comes out the lake is just like a sheet of glass, it's like a mirror. But at other times there's mist rising off the lake, and sometimes the tops of the mountains can't be seen at all. The wonderful thing about the view is that it changes constantly. It's a constant source of enjoyment.

# Unit 6　On the line

## 6A　Answerphone messages

### EXERCISES 1 and 2

1 Hi Jill, I'm so sorry I forgot to cancel the appointment with John Gregson. Um, can you ring him? Er, the number is 446–2437. Have you got that? 446–2437. Er, can you arrange the meeting for Wednesday lunchtime? That's the best time for me. OK, thanks. Bye.

2 Er, hello Jill, it's um Roger here. You remember, from the er holiday in Greece? Um, now you foolishly said that there might be a bed for the night if I was to be in London at all, and er well here I am, I'm in Victoria Station, actually. Well, I'm um, I'm just over the road from Victoria Station, the café. Um, what's the best thing? I think, I tell you what, I'll try you again in about half an hour. OK. Thanks a lot. Bye.

3 Hello, Mrs Brown. It's Whites the tailor here. About your coat – it's very nearly finished but I'm afraid I'm going to have to do one more fitting just to get the shoulders right. Could you call in tomorrow some time? Thank you very much.

4 Jill, it's Liz. It's not important. Um, I just rang to um see if we could meet for a drink some time this week. Um, I'll call you again this evening. Bye.

5 Hello, Jill? It's Steve here. Listen, I'm having a few people round to dinner on Friday at about 7.30. Can you come? It'd be great to see you. If you can, could you give me a call? Thanks very much. Bye.

6 Oh hello. This is a message for Jill Brown. Um, my name is Claire Dunne. I'm from the Children's Press. I saw your work at an exhibition in Glasgow and liked it very much. Er, we, we are producing a new series of children's books, and we'd be interested in using you to do some of the illustrations if that's possible. Um, i-if you're interested, could you ring us as soon as possible? The number is 041-289-3150. Er, that, if you ask for me, that's Claire Dunne, D-U-double N-E, that would be good. We look forward to hearing from you. Bye.

7 Um, hello Jill, it's um, it's Roger here, um Roger, Roger Warden again, I, I phoned before. Um, well I'm still at this café at

Victoria Station, um the trouble is it's getting a bit late and um, and I haven't made any other arrangements for where to stay tonight. Um, hum, I think um I'll just go out for a, for another walkabout, and um, look I'll definitely be back in the café by 8 o'clock, all right? If you can possibly meet me there, please do. All right, then. Thank you. Bye.

## 6B  Phone calls

### EXERCISES 1 and 2

1 Hello, 4147. Yes? . . . Hello, how are you? . . . Yes, I do . . . That's right, Peter's party, that's right, yes, yes. Well, how are you? What have you been doing? . . . Have you been working? . . . And where are you now? . . . Oh really? So you'll be staying here for some time? . . . Oh that's really good. Well, we must, we must meet up . . . This Saturday? . . . Ah, what a shame. Er, I think just this weekend I'm going to be away. I'm going off on Friday night, going off um up north for a few days . . . Oh that's really a shame . . . Well, yes, that would be really good. Yes, what's, have you got a telephone? . . . Yes . . . Yeah, 663, yes . . . 24, 2453. OK, well maybe I'll, I'll give you a ring when I come back after the weekend . . . That would be really nice. OK, well I'll ring you, I'll ring you at the beginning of next week. OK, yeah, that's pretty good . . . Well, I'll ring you next week then. Thank, thanks for ringing – it's really nice to hear from you. OK, bye.

2 Hello, 4147 . . . Pardon? . . . I'm sorry, who? . . . Er no, there's nobody called Jimmy living here . . . No, no, sorry, I think maybe you've got the wrong number. What number did you want? . . . No, sorry, it's 4147. OK, bye bye.

3 Hello, 4147 . . . You're back! . . . Oh, that's, that's really really good. And how was Italy? . . . Was it? . . . Was it? . . . Was it, was it worth going to? . . . Did you er . . . Were you at the conference all the time? . . . And how was your lecture? . . . So, do you think you might um, you might get some more work out of it? . . . Yeah . . . Oh, yes, yes. Hey look, why don't we um, why don't we have lunch together tomorrow and you can tell me all about it . . . Yeah. OK, well I'll meet you . . . Yes, OK, I'll meet you in the usual place in the café, OK? At about 1

o'clock? . . . That's a bit late . . . Yeah, OK make it 1.30, that would be really good. All right. It's lovely to hear from you. See you tomorrow. Bye.

4 Hello, 4147. Hello. How are you? . . . Oh that's good, yes . . . Yes . . . Yes . . . I was quite worried about you with all that rain, because I really thought that, er it must have been pretty awful on the motorway . . . Yes, but that's good that you're back already . . . Yes, it was lovely . . . Yes . . Yes . . . Well, I hope you er have a chance to recover, and you feel . . . Yes OK, right, I'll be down then, but I'll ring you later in the week, and um let you know exactly when I'm coming . . . Right, yes I'm feeling better already . . . OK, see you soon. Bye bye.

5 Hello, 4147 . . . Oh, how are you? . . . Yes . . . Yes, well I rang to see how you were, and er Joe said that you were still in bed, so . . . Really? Poor thing! It's been going on for quite a long time, hasn't it? . . . Did you see the doctor? . . . Yeah . . . Actually, I do know, I know several other people who have had it as well, it seems to take about two or three days to get over it all . . . Really? Well, maybe you, you should take it easy for a few days and recover . . . Anyway, um maybe we should put off er going swimming until next week, because . . . No, OK . . . Yeah, right . . . Right, well, why don't you just ring me whenever you feel better? That would be the best thing . . . OK . . . Yes, yes . . . No, just a bit of a cold, that's all. Right, I'll hear from you when you get better anyway . . . Yeah, look after yourself . . . OK, bye.

# Unit 7   Intruders

## 7A   Scare stories

### EXERCISE 1

*Story A*
Well, it happened a few years ago. I had to prepare myself for an examination at school, and I'm living in a house with my parents, and well, I was working in the basement at my table when my parents went shopping to the city, when I heard steps on the floor above me, and I knew there is actually no person in the house besides me, and what could that be? And I was terribly frightened because I knew that must be a burglar and we had the windows open to air

the room, and that must be a burglar, what to do?

*Story B*
I woke up in the middle of the night, and the curtains were slightly drawn back and there was this great thing flapping around in the room, and I was absolutely terrified, it was huge, and I realised that it was a bat, and I didn't know what to do because I had long hair in those days, and you know they always say that if you have long hair you must be careful of bats 'cause they'll get wound up in your hair.

## EXERCISE 3

*Story A*
*Section 1*
Well, it happened a few years ago. I had to prepare myself for an examination at school, and I'm living in a house with my parents, and well I was working in the basement at my table when my parents went shopping to the city, when I heard steps on the floor above me, and I knew there is actually no person in the house besides me, and what could that be? And I was terribly frightened because I knew that must be a burglar and we had the windows open to air the room, and that must be a burglar, what to do?

*Section 2*
And I remembered that I have a toy gun in my cupboard, um so I decided to take the toy gun and go upstairs. Well, I took the toy gun, went outside of my room and shouted as if there is another person, 'Steve, take the dogs and go outside.'

*Section 3*
And um then I went upstairs and made lots of lights in all the rooms, and then the burglar must have heard me, and he rushed out of the window the way he came in.

*Section 4*
Well, I was relieved then and then I tried to phone my parents, and I was so terribly frightened that I just wasn't able to dial the number.

*Story B*
*Section 1*
I woke up in the middle of the night, and the curtains were slightly drawn back and there was this great thing flapping around in the room, and I was absolutely terrified, it was huge, and I realised that it was a bat, and I didn't know what to do because I had long hair

in those days, and you know they always say that if you have long hair you must be careful of bats 'cause they'll get wound up in your hair.

*Section 2*
And I was absolutely petrified, and I put my head under the covers and waited, and when I looked out again it was still there, and I just didn't, I just didn't know what to do, it was terrifying.

*Section 3*
Um, well, in the end um, I er, I just dragged the clothes off the bed and got, went out of the room, and my friend was in the room next door, and I spent the night on the floor in her room.


## 7B   Jigsaw story

### EXERCISE 1

And I looked at him, and I didn't even think, I just felt so angry, I just rushed at him and fell on him.

Anyway I got up, I pulled on a house dress, and I'd just pulled on my dress and turned round when the door of my bedroom opened.

He dropped the bags and managed to wriggle his coat back on, and dashed out of the flat, with me rushing after him, screaming 'Stop, stop, stop.'

It was someone moving in all the rooms, and very quietly. And I was rather suspicious.

Yes, we heard you shouting, but we thought it was a domestic quarrel between your two flatmates, and we didn't want to interfere.

At that time my friends started teaching in the morning before I did.

And we struggled and wrestled all the way up the corridor of the flat towards the front door, with me trying to pull off his jacket just to stop him and me trying to get the bags out of his hands.

And when I woke up I became aware of sounds in the flat and I thought at first that it was my friends who'd come back from work.

And a man stood on the threshold holding two bulging plastic bags full of cameras and tape recorders and cassettes.

And Tariq, my colleague, came to the door, and

I said, 'A thief, a thief in our flat, didn't you hear me shouting?'

## EXERCISE 2

At that time my friends started teaching in the morning before I did. And when I woke up I became aware of sounds in the flat and I thought at first that it was my friends who'd come back from work. And then I began to think the sounds were rather strange because it wasn't someone just clattering happily round, moving plates, making a noise. It was someone moving in all the rooms, um very quietly. And I was rather suspicious. Anyway I got up, I pulled on a house dress, and I'd just pulled on my dress and turned round when the door of my bedroom opened and a man stood on the threshold holding two bulging plastic bags full of cameras and tape recorders and cassettes and any hardware that he could lay his hands on round the flat. And I looked at him, and I didn't even think, I just felt so angry, I just rushed at him and fell on him, and started trying to fight him and pull the bags away. And we struggled and wrestled all the way up the corridor of the flat towards the front door, with me trying to pull off his jacket just to stop him and me trying to get the bags out of his hands. Anyway at the door of the flat he decided to give up the struggle. He dropped the bags and managed to wriggle his coat back on, and dashed out of the flat, with me rushing after him, screaming 'Stop, stop, stop,' and and then banging on the nearest door er where one of our colleagues from the department lived. And Tariq, my colleague, came to the door and I said 'A thief, a thief in our flat, didn't you hear me shouting?' And he said, 'Oh sorry,' he said, 'Yes, we heard you shouting, but we thought it was a domestic quarrel between your two flatmates, and we didn't want to interfere.'

# Unit 8  Childhood

## 8A  *Buried treasure*

### EXERCISE 2

We set off, my eldest sister was about nine, the middle one seven, I suppose I would have been four. And we packed a picnic, we took some orange juice and a packet of biscuits, and we took tools for finding treasure, we took a sledgehammer and a pickaxe. And we set off across the fields, through the woods and up into another field, which was a ploughed field. And there in the ploughed field, at the edge of the ploughed field were all stones that the farmer had thrown to the edge of the field, so they, that they didn't break his plough. And my eldest sister Claire decided that there was gold in one of those stones. And so she handed the sledge-hammer to my sister Kate, who threw it back over her shoulder, and caught me square between the eyes, so I was knocked out, I was unconscious. Well, they thought they'd killed me, that I was dead, and what do you do with dead people? Well, you bury them. And so they rolled me into a ditch and covered me with branches and leaves and bits of earth and sat down to have a picnic. So they ate biscuits and drank orange juice, and talked about what they ought to tell my mother. At that point I came to again and groaned, and they dug me up and brushed me down and stood me on my feet, and taught me to say very loudly, 'I walked into a tree.' And that's what we told my mother, and that's what she still believes.

### EXERCISE 4

1  And we packed a picnic, we took some orange juice and a packet of biscuits.

2  And we took tools for finding treasure, we took a sledgehammer and a pickaxe.

3  At the edge of the ploughed field were all stones that the farmer had thrown to the edge of the field, so they, that they didn't break his plough.

4  And my eldest sister Claire decided that there was gold in one of those stones.

5  And so they rolled me into a ditch and covered me with branches and leaves and bits of earth and sat down to have a picnic.

6  They dug me up and brushed me down and stood me on my feet, and taught me to say very loudly, 'I walked into a tree.' And that's

what we told my mother, and that's what she still believes.

## 8B  *Party games*

**EXERCISES 2 and 3**

A  There's a game called 'Hunt the thimble', where one person goes out of the room, and then so- um somebody else hides a thimble, and the person has to come in and look for it. Um, and once they've found it, they just have to choose a different person. And it can be really anywhere where you hide the thing, as long as it's in one room.

B  There's this party game called 'Eat the chocolate'. And everyone sits down in a circle, and there's a dice, and in the middle of the circle there's a plate with a piece of chocolate, quite a large piece. And um there's a hat, pair of gloves, a scarf and a jacket which are placed in the middle of the circle as well. And each person gets a turn at throwing the dice. And if they get a six, they get dressed up in the hat, gloves, scarf and jacket, and they get to eat the chocolate, but they have to use a knife and fork. And sometimes they don't get enough time because the next person throws a six.

C  Well, everyone sits in a circle, and a bowl of eggs is put in the middle. Now half of these eggs are raw, and half of them are hard-boiled. And one by one everybody stands up and they have to crack this egg on their head very hard. And of course if it's raw it'll go all over them, but if it's hard-boiled then they'll be fine and they just sit back down. If you don't like getting messy, of course, then you can wear a towel round your shoulders and a bath cap on your head to keep your hair from getting all wet.

D  Well, you get in partners, and you have er two or one roll of toilet paper to each partner, and then you have a certain amount of time. And then everyone wraps one person up in toilet paper. And the first person that gets it all done, they win, and the neatest person. But if it's not neat then they don't win and it's the second person down.

# Unit 9  Bought and sold

## 9A  *Morning market*

**EXERCISES 2 and 3**

P:  You're tuned to Central Radio 94.5 FM, 23 minutes to twelve. Now let's see if Sue's there. Hello, Sue. (*Hello.*) Right, and how are you? (*Fine, thank you.*) OK, what can we do for you?

S:  Er, I've got a couple of keyboards for sale, one's a Yamaha C501, (*C501.*), and a mini-synthesiser (*Yeah.*) that's a battery one, er £30. (*OK, right.*) and next one's a Casio NT 205, and that's plus a mains unit. (*That's a keyboard?*) Yeah, that's right. (*Another keyboard.*) And that's £70.

P:  Right, Casio keyboard at £70, the Yamaha synthesiser, the C501, £30 for that.

S:  That's it, they're both with instruction booklets and er the original boxes as well. (*Good.*) and er the last thing is um a, a wardrobe, a veneer one, er 1950s thereabouts, that's £12.

P:  Right, wardrobe 50s style £12, Casio keyboard at £70, and the Yamaha C501 synthesiser £30. (*That's right.*) Right, let's have your number.

S:  312865.

P:  312865. Thank you, Sue. (*Thank you very much.*) Bye bye now. (*Bye.*) Now we've got Nick on the line. Hello, Nick. (*Hello, there.*) How can I help you?

N:  I've got three things for sale. (*Off you go, then.*) Um, a four foot dressing table, modern style, four drawers, £20. Um, an Indesit fridge, in working condition, ten years old, that's £30, and a six-string guitar with case, £25.

P:  Right, we've got three items there. Dressing table, £20, a fridge, an Indesit, £30 for that, and a guitar for £25. (*That's it.*) What's your number, Nick?

N:  It's 21260.

P:  All right, Nick. (*Cheers.*) Bye bye. (*Bye.*) 21260, that's the telephone number for dressing table, fridge and guitar. And our next caller today is Julie. Hello, Julie. (*Hello.*) You're selling something?

J:  Yes, I'm selling an English leather saddle, which is, well, it has a 40 centimetre seat, which is an adult size. (*Right.*) Right, it's for sale at £75, and please contact 613870.

P:  OK, that's 613870, an English leather saddle, 40 centimetre seat, it's an adult size, £75. Thank you, Julie. Bye bye. (*Bye.*) More calls on the 'Morning Market' in a few minutes' time, now it's 16 minutes to twelve.

## 9B  *What do you think of it?*

### EXERCISES 1 and 2

1 A: Oh, Richard, they look wonderful.
 B: Er, er hang on, they're not for you, they're for my girlfriend's mother. (*Oh.*) Yeah, I'm going to stay for the weekend. This is my sort of coming-to-stay present.
 A: Oh, they'll like those, they're wonderful.
 B: I hope so, they're jolly expensive, you know.
 A: Are they? How much?
 B: £5.99, just for, just for that much. (*Really? That is expensive.*) Mm, they'll all be gone in a day, I should think.
 A: They'll all be gone in an hour!

2 A: Yes, but what are you going to use it for?
 B: There are so many things you can use it for. You can use it for typing out letters and (*Yeah.*) storing the letters (*Yeah, but.*) for keeping bills, shopping lists.
 A: Yes, I suppose. So will you use it just at home or will you use it you know for office things as well?
 B: No, just, just for home use. (*Just for home.*)
 A: How much did it cost?
 B: Well, it was one of the cheapest ones. (*Yeah.*) Just over £1,000.

3 A: Look, Richard, what do you think of this? I bought it for Robbie, you know er my brother's little boy.
 B: Oh gosh, lovely, I used to have those when I was a kid, I remember. (*Good, isn't it?*) Does it work?
 A: Yes, yes, look, look, if you push it along then this little bit comes up here (*Right.*) and then you can hook things on the back, and er. (*And pull things along with it?*) Yeah.
 B: Mm, lovely. (*Good, isn't it?*)

4 A: You'll never guess what I've bought, Judy. (*What?*) Look at this.
 B: Oh, goodness. (*Isn't it splendid?*) It's wonderful. Where are you going to wear it, though?
 A: I'm going to wear it on the beach in Minorca. (*Oh!*) I'm going to stay with some old friends there. (*Very nice.*) So I thought this would keep the sun off me.

 B: Oh, it'll certainly do that.

5 A: Well, I saw it in the shop window and I thought 'I must have one.'
 B: Can I try it, can I just . . .?
 A: Well, hold on. The batteries go in the back here, (*Yeah.*) let me just show you, and it's got a radio, and you put your cassettes in the front there, and the little headphones plug in there, (*Fantastic.*) and it . . .
 B: Great, let me, let me have a . . .
 A: Right, let me just push the button . . . (*Yep*) Can you hear?
 B: Hey, fantastic!
 A: It's good, isn't it?

# Unit 10  Behind the picture

## 10A  *Blackhouse*

### EXERCISE 2

This house is er is in fact my house 100 years ago, when it was a blackhouse. This house is in Glenelg, which is in the Highlands of Scotland. And this family in front of it are tinkers. Um, tinkers are like gypsies, er they wander about and they make things and they sell them. They're selling pots and buckets which they make themselves.

In this photograph they are in front of a blackhouse, which is a very very, well, this photograph is 100 years old, and at that time er, most of the houses in the Highlands were blackhouses, which were thatched and built of stone, usually quite long buildings because part of the house was for the animals, so that the family lived in one part, and the animals lived in the other half.

And um the thing about the blackhouses is that they were called blackhouses because they were so smoky inside, um because they had, the fire was usually in the middle, and the smoke curled up and out of a small hole in the roof, and they really were very smoky, you couldn't er you couldn't really see very well inside.

### EXERCISE 3

Someone found these photographs in an album, a very old album in a bookshop, and came to visit all the places where the photographs were taken. Er, he came into my workshop and showed us the photographs, and then brought this photograph out, and said, 'This is my most favourite photograph. I wonder where it is in Glenelg.' And I said, 'It could be anywhere, in fact it could be here,' and then we went out and we looked up and down the road, and we looked at the other photographs he had and we saw the houses on either side, and we realised that it was actually the house.

## 10B  The Scream

### EXERCISE 2

This picture is 'The Scream' by Edvard Munch, and it's a very powerful picture, it's in black and white as as you see it here. And um I think it's particularly powerful because mainly because of that figure who um, who is, who seems to be running off this bridge here holding his or her head in her hands and screaming. And um, what's very interesting about the picture are the two, the two figures at the end of the bridge or further up this road. And it's difficult to understand whether the person is running from them or whether they're just er innocent bystanders.

Um, so the reason I, I like this picture, the reason I find it powerful is because I think that the person is not actually running from the two dark figures at the end of the bridge, but in fact the person is suffering er perhaps some kind of terrible loneliness or sadness, and is, actually seems to be trying to hide that feeling from those people. And I think this is a common feeling, I think this is something which we all do sometimes when, when we feel some feeling, usually a bad feeling, something like loneliness or terrible unhappiness, we don't want other people to see that, and er so we, we have to try and hide that feeling from, from other members of the, of the public. And I feel that's what this man or woman is doing in the picture here.

### EXERCISE 3

As a design, the picture's very strong as well. The, the bridge or the street is a very strong diagonal line which goes through the, the picture. And then to the, to the right of the screamer's head there's a series of dark vertical lines – it's difficult to know what that is, perhaps it's a field or maybe it could be a wall, it's difficult to know exactly what it is, but those dark vertical lines somehow depress the picture, which is exactly what the artist wanted. And then at the, at the top, you have the sky, which the artist has, has er made in the form perhaps of clouds, which are very strong horizontal lines, very, very bold black lines which again seem to push the whole picture down, and add to the depression of the, the

experience which the, the screamer is er, is feeling.

# Unit 11    Believe it or not

## 11A    Macbeth

### EXERCISE 2

In the theatre there's one superstition that everyone knows, which is that you should not mention the name of the play by Shakespeare – 'Macbeth'. It's called 'The Scottish Play' if you want to talk to someone about it, or 'That play' or 'Mac- oh I'm not supposed to say it', which often happens. But if you do say the word 'Macbeth' by mistake, there are several ways you can break the spell – you can make the superstition not have any terrible effect. If you say it in the, in the dressing room, you should leave the dressing room, turn round three times in a clockwise direction, swear, and then knock on the door and ask to be let back into the room. And only until someone says 'Come in' can you go back in again. Otherwise you have to leave the theatre. Um, a lot of people shrug it off, say they don't believe it, but most people will stick to the rules of not saying it.

### EXERCISE 4

The reasons I think that it, it has become a superstition is because there are an awful lot of accidents that have happened during various productions of Macbeth. One awful one was when a shield during one of the fights was thrown mistakenly off stage and beheaded a member of the audience. There have been other occurrences of people actually getting stabbed during some of the fight scenes and Lady Macbeth catching fire during the sleepwalking scene. And nobody wants these to happen during their production or their play, whether it's Macbeth or not, so they prefer not to say the word 'Macbeth' in a theatre.

## 11B    Palm reading

### EXERCISE 2

1 Well, you've got a very interesting hand, in fact. Um, it looks as though you're a very determined character. Um, you've got a very strong head line, um your heart line goes down quite a lot, there's quite a strong connection between the two, so I think there either have been or will be two women in your life. And it looks as though during your

early life um you either were ill or you changed your mind about the way, the direction in which your life was going to go. Um, it looks to me as though you're a fairly artistic person, um, yes, I would, I would say very artistic.

2 Now let's have a look at your hand here. Now you've got a very square, very practical hand, so you're somebody who's not afraid of hard work. On the other hand, you've got a very strange line of imagination with lots of little, little wrinkles, little valleys coming off it, which means that you're also a very imaginative person as well as being very practical. Coming down here from just above your thumb is your, is your life line. And it starts off in a little, little vaguely, it's not a very well defined line, and this I think would indicate that at the beginning of your life you weren't very sure where you wanted to go, what you wanted to do, but then gradually when you got to about your twenties, I would say, you suddenly take off in this direction very, very firmly indeed, and this goes right on, I think this would, would tell me that you're going to go on in your present career until you retire at actually I have to tell you quite an early age. And just coming out of that line and going right across your hand, you've got, it's probably what we would call endeavour and determination, and I have to tell you that this again is a line that is not very firm and deep, it's a little bit vague and a little bit wavy, and I think that means that you're somebody who questions themselves a lot and is never absolutely sure that what they're going to do is right or not. And that doesn't get better as you go through life.

# Unit 12   Bread and mushrooms

## 12A   Making bread

### EXERCISE 2

1 Um, first thing is to prepare the yeast. If you use fresh yeast, er you mix it with some sugar and the yeast goes a little bit liquid, then you add a little water or milk or water and milk, um and leave it, leave it till it's all bubbly, and about twice as, the volume that it was.

2 And then mix it into the flour. Mix in the yeast, and gradually mix in the liquid – again it might be water, it might be milk and water.

And mix this until you've got something which is sticky, but not very sticky.

3 At that point take it out of the bowl and start kneading – kneading is when you push it around, and you push it into shape, you pull it out of shape, and you push it into shape and you pull it again. And keep on doing this, um ooh five or ten minutes usually, until it feels, you can feel it's really springy.

4 And then roll it up, roll it into a ball and leave it. It's ready when it's double the size it was when you left it, but you can leave it really as long as you like.

5 Come back, knead it again and then start shaping it. Um, push it into the shape you want it, again let it rise, and then put it in a very, very hot oven, very, very hot, and start bringing the temperature down.

6 And white bread, I forget, I think it takes about 20 minutes, and then to see whether it's done you tip it out of the tin, give it a tap, and if you get a sort of hollow sound then you know, yeah that's the bread.

## 12B   Edible or poisonous?

### EXERCISES 2 and 3

Well, this little one here, this is the um the field mushroom. Er you'll recognise this from, from supermarkets. It's, it's very good to eat and it's the mushroom that is most commonly sold in, in shops. It's easy to recognise, it's got a white, slightly brownish cap, um and a white stem, and you can see this little skirt around the stem here. Underneath, some pinkish brown gills. Um it's called the field mushroom because it, it grows in fields, especially where there are animals like horses or sheep.

Now here's a very different one, a very beautiful mushroom called the fly agaric. It's also very easy to recognise, it has this bright red cap with, with tiny white spots on it. Again it's got a white stem with a little skirt around it. This mushroom is actually highly poisonous, and it contains a drug that, that gives you hallucinations, so um best not to eat them. You'll find them growing, growing near trees, not in fields.

Now here's another mushroom that grows near trees. A very different mushroom, this one, it's extremely good to eat, some people say it's the, the most delicious of all mushrooms, and it's called the cep. And you'll see it has this, it's a very large mushroom with a, with a smooth brown cap, a shiny cap, it looks as if it's wet, and this big thick stem, with no skirt on it. And underneath you'll see it doesn't have gills, it, it has these, these white or yellow pores, which look very much like a sponge. That's a, that's a really lovely mushroom to eat.

And this last one is very definitely not a good mushroom to eat. Um, it's called the death cap, and it's the most poisonous of all mushrooms. You need to eat only one of these and it will very probably kill you. It's a very dangerous mushroom this, because it grows under trees, and it actually looks quite harmless. Um, it's got this white greenish cap, a whitish green stem, and again a skirt around the stem very much like the field mushroom has, but you can tell that it's the poisonous death cap because it's got this white bag at the bottom of the stem. So always look for this, this white bag, and if it, if it's got one, er then don't eat that mushroom.

# Unit 13   Learning to draw

## 13A   *The right side of your brain*

### EXERCISE 2

A: A lot of people think that they can't draw. I don't think that I can draw, but you obviously feel that you'd be able to teach most people to draw in some sort of way.

B: That's right. Um, everybody can learn how to draw. And I tell you why that is. Most people simply don't use their brain the right way.

### EXERCISE 3

B: A brain is like a walnut, with two halves, a left side and a right side. The left-hand side we use for language, we speak with that side, we read, we make sums, do calculations, keep time, all the kind of practical sides, and as a result that's the side most people use most of the time. The right-hand side is the imaginary side, the side we use for dreaming, for um enjoying abstract things maybe like colours and nature, and that kind of things. It's also the side we use for drawing. What you must learn to be able to see like an artist is to shift from the left side to the right side, and that is something everybody can learn.

### EXERCISE 4

A: So how do you move from using one side of the brain to using the other side?

B: Well, it's just a question of learning to reuse that side, because we all used the right side when we were children, and everybody could draw without worry everything that they wanted to draw. And then when you're about 12 suddenly you want to draw it exactly right, as what you think is exactly right, and discover you can't do it any more, and stop drawing, so you have to learn again to use your brain in that free and open way.

A: Why is it that children stop using that side of the brain? What happens to them at that age to make them stop using both sides of their brain?

B: They go to secondary school, and they suddenly have to do lots of homework, lots of mathematical things, and their whole education is geared towards using the left side, and the right side is simply not considered important.

## 13B   *A drawing exercise*

### EXERCISE 2

You see that drawing. It's upside down. Now don't turn it round till you've finished this exercise, and that's important. Are you ready? Take a pencil and a paper.

You're going to copy this drawing, but you're starting at the top of the drawing, and don't think about what it is, don't name the things, simply move from line to line. Look at the line in relation to another line, like a jigsaw puzzle, put the pieces together.

Work your way slowly through the drawing, and once you've started to draw, you'll find that you become very interested in how those lines go together. Just look at the lines, and take your time. Look at the spaces between them. Everything you have to know is there right in front of your eyes. Just continue to copy. Move from one line to another.

### EXERCISE 3

Have you finished your drawing? Then you can turn the book upside down. The drawing in it becomes now the right way up. Compare the two drawings. How does that look? Now you see that everybody can learn how to draw.

# Unit 14  Male and female

## 14A  Men and women

### EXERCISES 2 and 3

A: It seems to me women are much better at dealing with more than one thing at a time, and whether this is actually to do with the difference in their brain or whether it's er just how they have to cope more often with more than one thing, for example, it is usually women who work, have babies, look after the babies and take main responsibility for looking after the home. And maybe it's practising all that that makes women better able to do more than one thing at a time. Men, it seems to me, can only concentrate on one thing at a time, including boring domestic things like washing the dishes. If a friend of mine who's a man washes the dishes he'll find it quite difficult to conduct a conversation even at the same time, whereas if I'm doing the dishes I'm always washing the dishes, talking to someone, probably cooking something as well, and finding that not too stressful.

B: Do you think that there are things that men are naturally better at than women?

A: Again I would have um said no, but perhaps now I think they are maybe better at er concrete things.

B: One example that I've read about is that men are better at things like reading maps, they're better at geography than women.

A: I know, I know one man who's very bad at reading maps, most other men I know are, like maps, I think that's it too, they actually enjoy the um, I think it's to do with trapping the universe on a piece of paper, and to do with wanting to reduce things to something easily understandable whereas women are loath to um, to actually look at the world and think 'Yes, we can write it down on a piece of paper.'

B: Do you think women are more interested in personal relationships than men?

A: Generally, yes, though again whether this is because from an early age they're taught to please other people, whereas men are taught to please themselves, I think. I think relationships are more central to most women's lives. For example, I think men don't have very good conversations with each other, whereas women do. If you eavesdrop or listen to women talking, often they'll be having, after a relatively short time of knowing each other, fairly personal and truthful conversations, whereas men are very, they have conversations not about what I'd call real things. They'll talk about their work in a very superficial way, or their interests in a very superficial way, for example, and football is the um, just a sort of way of men to relate to each other without actually saying anything important, it seems to me.

## 14B  Girls and boys

### EXERCISE 2

1 I've helped at a playgroup as well recently, and I've noticed that er the boys take up all the space. The girls end up playing in a little, they have a house corner, and the girls end up in the house corner, or over in the book corner, which are clearly defined spaces where boys don't run around, whereas the rest of the space is taken up by boys running around um, attacking each other, being Superman or Batman.

2 I think generally that er, the way boys play tends to be more um, aggressive, perhaps even more violent than the way that girls play. Boys, for example, tend to play games which involve competition, particularly they may use some kind of weapon, a sword or a gun. On the other hand, girls tend to play more cooperatively, and I think more peacefully.

3 I think the boys tend to like playing war games, er doing a lot more sort of physical things, whereas girls will tend to play a lot more games like skipping and games that are focussed around babies and teddy bears and things like that.

### EXERCISE 3

**A**

At this particular playgroup one of the teachers there is particularly lenient towards the boys, and channels the girls into corners. And I noticed a little girl was playing with a train the other day, and a little boy who was slightly younger than her wanted it. And she said, 'Oh, you go and play with the doll in the corner because Douglas wants the train.' And that was her being taught already to give way to the boy's wishes.

**B**

I think that boys wish to copy or identify with other males, and girls wish to copy or identify with other females. So in the case of girls, particularly very young girls, they often see their mother in a very domestic situation and therefore they copy the things that their mother does, which tend to be domestic and often tend to involve babies. Boys perhaps see less of their father because the father is very often out working. So perhaps a very large influence for young boys would come from television, where of course they see often a fairly violent type of male image. Men on television are shown as, for example, as cowboys or as policemen or as superheroes.

**C**

I have found from my own experience with my own son that up until he started nursery, that actually he used to play lots of games that girls and boys would have played. But I think that once he became involved with larger peer groups and started watching television that that influenced a great deal what he plays now, and I've noticed that with a lot of other children. And I notice that boys tend to play these games of re-enacting the television programmes, they tend to copy what they see on television that men and boys should do.

# Unit 15    Bees

## 15A    Life in the hive

### EXERCISE 2

The queen has only one function and that's to lay eggs. The worker, the workers have different jobs at different stages in their life. When they hatch they become nurse bees, and they simply look after the eggs and the growing um, the, the bees which are still in cells, and they feed them and they keep them clean and they keep them warm. Um, and then as they grow older they become guard bees, and that means they stand around outside and inside the entrance to the hive, um to protect the hive from attack of any kind. And then in the last phase of their life they become forager bees, and they're the ones that fly out and find the nectar, which they turn into honey. Not for us really, we steal their honey, the honey is really to feed, to keep themselves alive.

Um, and the drones are the male bees. Their only function is to mate with the queen, um and, and they die at that point. And at the end of the summer, the bees push the drones out into the cold, and you find piles of dead drones round the hive, because they're just extra mouths to feed during the winter.

## 15B    Catching a swarm

### EXERCISE 2

The first thing you hear is a huge noise, it's the biggest noise you've ever heard in your life. All the bees come out, and the sound of their wings makes this great humming sound. Um, and from that point you've got to work quite quickly. Usually what happens is that the swarm settles on a branch of a bush or a tree quite close to the hive, um and it looks like a great big black football hanging there.

And what you must do is run very quickly and get your beekeeping clothes um, and climb into your overalls, your boots, your hat with the veil and your gloves. Um, and then if you've got a spray you should fill the spray with sugar and water and you hurry down to where the swarm is hanging on the branch, and you squirt the bees with sugar and water, and this um takes their mind off what you're about to do. Then you must find a cardboard box and a sheet, and you hold the cardboard box in your left hand, and put it under put, put the swarm of bees into the cardboard box. And with your right hand you shake the branch sharply, and the swarm falls into the box. And you then cover it very quickly with the sheet. Then you must find a cool place, and put the box and the bees in the cool place and wait till evening, when the sun goes down.

Meanwhile, you build a new hive. And into the hive you put some honey, so that the bees will think it's, um it's, it's like home. And when the sun goes down you put a board sloping up towards the entrance to the hive. Then very quickly you take the sheet off the cardboard box and tip the bees, the whole swarm out onto the board.

And then a very magic thing happens. As you stand and watch, all the bees turn and point with their heads up towards the door of the hive, and gradually but increasingly faster and faster they run up the board and into the door of the hive. And it takes about ten minutes um for all the bees um to go into their new home.

# Unit 16   Emergency

## 16A   Healthline

### EXERCISE 2

This tape describes the symptoms of heart attacks, and gives advice about what to do if someone suffers a heart attack.

Most heart attacks are caused by a blockage of one of the coronary arteries by a blood clot. This cuts off the blood supply to part of the heart muscle, which then dies. The main symptom of a heart attack is a tight pain in the chest, which may spread to one or both shoulders and down the arms to the hands.

Heart attacks vary greatly in their nature. They may occur suddenly with little or no warning, or they may develop gradually. The pain can vary from a slight feeling of discomfort to a very strong bursting feeling in the chest. It may last for up to an hour, or it may disappear after a few minutes and then return. A person suffering a heart attack is also likely to feel sick, dizzy and out of breath.

### EXERCISES 3 and 4

A heart attack is a serious matter and should be treated as an emergency. Don't try to travel to the doctor yourself, but stay with the patient and call an ambulance immediately. Keep the patient warm and as calm as possible. While you are waiting for help to arrive, lift the patient into a half sitting position. Put pillows or cushions behind the patient's head and neck, bend the knees and loosen any tight clothing around the neck, chest and waist. Don't give anything to eat or drink, and don't leave the patient alone. If the patient becomes unconscious, try mouth-to-mouth artificial respiration, and at the same time press down on the patient's chest to force blood around the body.

When the ambulance arrives, the patient will be taken straight to hospital, and will probably be kept there for several days. The patient's chances of recovery are very good: two out of every three people who have a heart attack recover completely, and nearly half a million people recover from heart attacks in Britain every year.

Thank you for calling.

## 16B   Street incident

### EXERCISE 2

*Section 1*
I remember when I really had to act in an emergency and that happened on November 5th night in South Kensington in London. And I was in a car at a set of traffic lights waiting to move forward and fireworks were going off all over the place, and I heard a bang and I looked off to my right and I just saw a lady collapsing by a bus stop.

*Section 2*
And I thought 'That lady's been shot'. I don't know why I thought that, but she had been. So I got out of the car, right there in the middle of the street, and went across to the bus stop, and indeed she'd been shot through the head. And as she fell to the ground I'd seen somebody dash off around Onslow Square but I couldn't chase them, I was more interested in the lady.

*Section 3*
Anyway there wasn't an awful lot I could do for her, but I ran along the road to a hotel and banged on the door and asked them to go and get the police or to bring an ambulance, and went back to the lady. And I remember when I came back to the lady at the bus stop, people were continuing to walk right past her, and they didn't take any notice of her, and there she was bleeding in the middle of the street.

*Section 4*
Anyway, I knelt down by the side of her, there wasn't an awful lot I could do. And just like there was in the films, somebody rolled down a window in a car, and they said 'Do you want a doctor?' and I said 'Yes'. And out of this car came a doctor, and he was able to keep her alive by giving her mouth-to-mouth resuscitation.

# Unit 17   Punishing children

## 17A   Smacking

### EXERCISE 1

A: Nine out of ten parents smack their children according to a report published today. But many of them also feel that smacking is wrong. The report carried out by the magazine 'Children' also claimed that parents often misunderstand their children's bad behaviour. Jenny Wright the editor of

'Children' is here with me now. Jenny, according to your report nine out of ten parents smack their children. What else did the report say?

B: Well, although about nine out of ten parents use smacking as a punishment, half of them feel guilty about using it. Well, the other half do smack their children and think they are right. It seems most parents we talked to smack their children more than once a week and five per cent actually smack their children every day.

A: Now you say in the report that parents should make more effort to understand their children and that smacking isn't always the best solution if children are naughty.

B: Yes, indeed. Yes, we feel if parents tried harder to understand, well how their children feel and why they react in certain ways, for example they might be jealous of a new baby brother or, or a sister or they might feel insecure, any, any number of things might make the child react badly.

A: So in those kinds of situations it would be better not to smack children?

B: Yes, yes, obviously, because when a child's behaving badly it needs love and attention, not anger and violence. I think parents should think really carefully before they smack their children.

A: Thank you, Jenny. That was Jenny Wright of 'Children' magazine.

## EXERCISE 2

1 I think talking to them, trying to explain why you're upset, what it is they have done wrong is better than hitting them, because if you hit them they learn to hit other things, other people, you, and I don't think that that is a solution to anything.

2 My experience as, as a mother now is you can, you can talk with a child very much and, and the child is going to understand much more than you believe, even if it is a one-year-old or two-years-old child. And I think it's um it's a very bad thing punishing children, because it remains being er an awfully dark er experience, and so it was it for me too, because when I'm thinking about my parents I can't help thinking about these days where they punished me.

3 Well, there's smacking and smacking. I don't at all agree with beating a child, but I do think sometimes a quick, short smack on the hand or arm is better than a long drawn-out moan. It's quick and the child understands it.

4 I can't really defend it when I, when I hit my child, I don't do it often but something about it makes me think that it's not a terrible thing to do. I mean, what are the alternatives? You can shout at your child, you can try to sit down and reason with your child, which is incredibly difficult if you're trying to talk to a two-year-old. Or what else can you do? You can send them out of the room, you can send them up to their room, you can not let them have any pudding for their dinner, or something, but I mean to me a little spank, to me it's quick, it's honest, it's physical, but having said all that I still try not to do it.

## 17B  Zen and the art of punishment

### EXERCISE 1

I have a Chinese friend whose father was a very famous Chinese traditional painter with brush and ink, black ink. And in my friend's family the only punishment for children when they did something naughty was to go and practise their Chinese calligraphy, that's writing Chinese characters with a brush and ink.

### EXERCISE 2

And before you start to do that you have to make the liquid ink by grinding a solid block of ink with water. You do that with your left hand, and that's very rhythmic. And then when you've made enough ink you start to draw or to write. And my friend says that when you have the brush just about um a couple millimetres from the paper, you can imagine in your eye, in your mind, the perfect stroke that you're going to make, it's going to be just perfect. And you can almost feel it going down your arm into your hand where you're holding the brush. But the moment the brush touches the paper you realise that you haven't done the perfect one, that there's something wrong with it. So then you lift the brush and you try again, and you try again and you try again.

### EXERCISE 3

And he says that as a punishment this is perfect, because after about five minutes you have forgotten the bad thing that you did, you've forgotten your anger at being caught, you've forgotten any injustice if you're being punished for something you haven't done, that all you're thinking about is reaching this perfection, reaching this state of drawing the perfect line. And very often you just forget, you'll stay for a very long time, even children will stay for a long time doing this, it becomes very peaceful um, so it sounds a much better form of punishment than, than violence, doesn't it?

# Unit 18  Planet Earth

## 18A  Traffic

### EXERCISES 2 and 3

A: Right, our first caller is Frederick Bowles. Are you there, Mr Bowles? (*Yes, I am.*) Good morning. (*Good morning.*) And er what have you got to say on the subject of traffic pollution?

B: Well, I think there are too many private cars on the road. Now that is what causes traffic congestion and also pollution. Now the way to solve the problem in my opinion isn't to build more roads. We should be improving our public transport instead – um more buses, more railways, maybe shared taxis.

A: I see, so Mr Bowles thinks that the government should spend less money on building more roads, and more money on improving public transport. Er, Barbara Fielding, what do you have to say to that?

C: Well, Mr Bowles, hello. Er, you're obviously not aware the government is spending money on on some forms of public transport. Er, for example, um some train services have been improved. But most people want to use their cars, Mr Bowles, so the government needs to spend most money on improving the roads, that's where the biggest problems are.

B: Well, Mrs Fielding, I think the government should do something more positive to discourage people from using their cars. Why not make people who use the roads pay a bit more?

C: Well, Mr Bowles I really can't agree with you there. It just isn't fair to make driving something that only rich people can afford. Many people need to use their cars, er, they're dependent on them, particularly those in the country.

A: Right, thank you very much, we'll leave that point for the moment and go on to our next caller if we may, who is Joanna Briggs. Hello, Joanna.

D: Oh, er hello, um well I think that the real problem is pollution. I mean, if we all carry on polluting the atmosphere like we are now we'll end up in the end destroying the whole planet. And I think it it's just stupid the way the government are putting more and more money into roads, because that just makes the whole problem worse. I mean, what what they should be doing, is they should be um doing everything they can to make people stop using their cars.

A: I see. What do you think they should be doing, for example, um besides what we've already discussed?

D: Well, um I think that um that really they've got to do something quite drastic like um, um limiting parking in towns, and in cities making the roads narrower instead of wider, because the wider the road is the more cars will come, and um and make the city centres um just for pedestrians and buses, no cars at all. And then this'll make people stop using their cars in the towns altogether because you know it'll simply be um too difficult and the parking will, will be too expensive for them.

A: I see. Er, Mrs Fielding.

C: Well, Joanna, it is very easy to say all that. But er in a modern society you just can't stop people using their cars, I mean after all the whole economy would collapse. No, no, no. The government is trying to improve roads. Now this helps people get to work faster. So people spend less time in their cars, and of course this therefore causes less pollution. That is the only realistic answer.

## 18B  Inside the greenhouse

### EXERCISE 2

A: Is the Earth really getting warmer?

B: There's no doubt at all that the Earth is getting warmer. Scientists, people who know about these things, tell us it is true, that four years out of the last ten have been the hottest since records began. And so if this effect – the greenhouse effect – continues, it's fairly certain, scientists believe, that within the next century, the next hundred years, the Earth will have heated up by four degrees. Yes, it is getting warmer.

### EXERCISE 3

A: But why does it matter if the world gets warmer?

B: It matters because it changes a lot of things

to do with our everyday life. If the Earth gets hotter, this will cause the level of the sea to rise by roughly between one and one-and-a-half metres over the next hundred years. It doesn't sound much – it's an awful lot. It'll cause flooding – vast areas of the Indian coast, Bangladesh, Holland, London even, will be under water.

A: And would there be any other effects?

B: There will be many other effects. One of the things that will happen is that we will have more storms. This will cause an awful lot of damage – damage to crops, to houses and to people. And there is another way that the world and our lives will be affected in this way, that certain areas of the world – America, the United States of America, and Russia – that grow an awful lot of the food for the world, could suffer from drought. And so if they're not making the food, there'll be famine – that's the problem. Areas like the Mediterranean, for example, could be turned into desert. We could simply not have enough to eat because the Earth is warming up.

# Unit 19    Sporting moments

## 19A    White water rafting

### EXERCISES 2 and 3

We went white water rafting in er Costa Rica. Um it was, Costa Rica, of course, is full of marvellous mountain rivers and beautiful tropical forests. I think it's one of the most beautiful countries I've ever visited. We, we took the landrover right up into the hills, and er we stood on the banks of this horrific-looking river, all brown and fierce and full of cruel-looking rocks. And we, and there were two rubber rafts, and we had two experts, one for each raft. And there were eight of us, that's seven untried people and, seven learners and one guide or expert in each raft. And we did everything in stages, because there would be one sort of fall and then a quiet pool, and then another huge fall and then another quiet pool. And so before we did the first, as it were descent, er the guides told us 'Watch out for that en- big tree branch that juts out over the river, because if you don't duck your heads as you go past it, you go past at such a rate that you'll knock yourselves out.' So we said 'Yes, yes, of course.' By the way we were all wearing

helmets, of course, er safety helmets rather like motorcyclists wear. So we started off and we shot down this um hillock of water, this kind of hill of water, brown foaming water, and the experience was so exciting and so tremendous that I completely forgot about the tree branch, and I went smash into it with my head, but of course the helmet protected me. But I felt such a total fool, you know, what what a start. But it was a most, it was a most amazing feeling, it was very, very, very exhilarating.

## 19B    Match of the day

### EXERCISES 2 and 4

1 Today ends with a fight featuring Onokuni, also known as the Panda. He has quite an easy fight today in a match against Fujino shin. Fujino shin is heavy at 150 kilos, rather close to the ground. He's nicknamed The Truth, which comes from a fighting name which means 'The True Mount Fuji'.

The fight is delayed by a false start from Fujino shin. That worries Onokuni a little – he's a man who doesn't like to start too soon.

It's the Panda who wins in the end. Fujino shin starts well, and he pushes the Panda backwards, but he doesn't seem to be able to follow through. Onokuni is just too big to move – and in the end he pushes his way through, using the advantage of 60 extra kilos and he carries Fujino shin away. A good win for Onokuni.

2 Now then, Higuita's come about 40 metres out of the goal there to take the ball. And he must be a worried man. Well, the atmosphere is really alight now here in Naples. Roger Milla, for Cameroon, hoping to get them through to the quarter final. No African country has ever gone that far. But it's not over yet. Can they do it again? Higuita comes out from the goal – seems to want to get involved, I do not believe it, a goal, he's thrown the chance away. Roger Milla scores – that's it, two nil. Roger Milla makes this World Cup belong to Cameroon. They now know that they're on the way I'm sure to the quarter finals. Higuita looks upset, the Colombians can't believe it.

3 And in first place is Glenda Walsh from the United States, then Kostic from Yugoslavia, and then comes Murray. But Murray is looking very comfortable indeed. And only 80 metres to go now, here comes Murray,

coming up past Kostic now, it's Walsh leading, Murray in second place. And Murray responds to the cheers of the crowd – with 80 metres to go, here she comes. Anne Murray hits the front, Walsh is beaten, and Anne Murray is going to win for Scotland. Here she is, she's over the line in one minute 44.96 seconds, and second was Glenda Walsh, but that was a good win for Anne Murray, under one minute 45 seconds, and this is only her second serious outdoor race this summer, she is looking very good.

# Unit 20    War zones

## 20A    *Arrival in Beirut*

### EXERCISES 2 and 3

I can remember coming into Beirut in the late 1970s, landing at the airport and seeing a big sign up across the top of it in both English and French, er saying 'Welcome to Beirut'. And then getting out of the plane and just being almost immediately surrounded by jeeps and people in uniforms with guns. Er, they were usually smiling, I didn't feel particularly threatened, there were just more than I'd ever seen before in one place. And then going into the arrivals lounge, which is usually a relatively empty place while you wait for your baggage – in Beirut it was crowded with people. People, not only people from the plane or customs officials, but people who had come in from outside in, past the customs officers to greet their friends or their relatives. And people all the time coming up to you, and asking if you wanted a taxi, or asking if you wanted somebody to help change money for you or to carry your bags or to help you through the customs. Just a constant noise and movement of people. And because the place wasn't very well signposted, I found I was often quite glad to accept help from some of these people, at least to show me which, which direction I ought to be going. And in general I found the atmosphere pretty friendly and not, not as tense as I'd expected it to be.

## 20B    *Northern Ireland*

### EXERCISE 2

A:  You're from Northern Ireland, but you've been living in Britain for quite some time. When you go back, what are the main things that you notice about everyday life in Northern Ireland?

B:  Well, I think largely it's very similar to the everyday life that you and I would have here, like the people go to school, they go to work, they stay at home with their children, you know that they do ordinary everyday things. And essentially on the surface, it would look like it's really quite normal. Although I think there's still quite a high presence of soldiers and police around various cities and towns, not quite as much as there was when I left 12 years ago. But essentially you know just walking through a town or city you know in the middle of the day, it would appear really quite normal.

A:  But that's on the surface. (*Yeah*.) How much has the fighting really changed people's lives?

B:  Well, I think it, it's really drastically changed them, in that people are living constantly with the threat of violence, death, um intimidation, murder, all you know, every single day, that that really does pervade people's lives, and it pervades everybody's home. I think people are living with an incredible level of terror all the time, and that because of that, I think it's very, very hard for even Ire- you know Irish people, Northern Irish people living at home to really be aware of it. It's like most people don't really want to see it, most people don't really want to talk about it. You know, when I talk to my family about it, they just say well it's, you know, we just live our lives, we just get on and do the things that we want to do, and it doesn't really affect us that much. You know, it's so painful to actually look at it, really what's happening. You know that people are being killed and maimed, you know, and terrorised in their own homes, and that to really look at that means taking on a lot of painful emotions, and I think people don't have the resources to do that.

A:  Do you think that people from other countries really appreciate what life is actually like in Northern Ireland?

B:  I don't think that people really do, no, and I think that people don't really want to know. There's, you know, the media and television display a certain part of life in the north of Ireland, and I think that actually that's just a very minimal part of it. And that people don't really appreciate things like the absolute beauty of the north of Ireland. People are very frightened to go and visit it. People, you know, they think they're going to get shot or murdered, and actually, you know, that is very unlikely. And I think that it's very important for people, if they really want to find out about the north of Ireland to go and visit it, to go and see people living there, to see that life is actually really quite normal, but at the same time to appreciate the beauty of the north of Ireland and the tragedy of the war situation happening there and still going on today.

## EXERCISE 3

1 Well, I think largely it's very similar to the everyday life that you and I would have here, like the people go to school, they go to work, they stay at home with their children, you know that they do ordinary everyday things.

2 And essentially on the surface, it would look like it's really quite normal. Although I think there's still quite a high presence of soldiers and police around various cities and towns.

3 and 4 Well I think it, it's really drastically changed them, in that people are living constantly with the threat of violence, death, um intimidation, murder, all you know, every single day, that that really does pervade people's lives, and it pervades everybody's home.

5 It's like most people don't really want to see it, most people don't really want to talk about it. You know, when I talk to my family about it, they just say well it's, you know, we just live our lives, we just get on and do the things that we want to do, and it doesn't really affect us that much.

6 There's, you know, the media and television display a certain part of life in the north of Ireland, and I think that actually that's just a very minimal part of it.

7 and 8 And that people don't really appreciate things like the absolute beauty of the north of Ireland. People are very frightened to go and visit it. People, you know, they think they're going to get shot or murdered, and actually, you know, that is very unlikely.

# To the teacher

This book further develops the approach to listening featured in *Listening 1*. It has two main aims:
— to provide *opportunities* to listen to a wide variety of natural spoken English, presented in a way that is accessible to learners;
— to develop students' listening *skills* by helping them to draw on their own natural strategies for listening effectively.

## Listening strategies

A fundamental idea underlying this book is that listening is not merely a 'passive' or 'receptive' skill; rather that when we listen we naturally employ a variety of active 'strategies' which help us to make sense of what we are listening to.

These strategies include:
— making predictions about what the speaker is going to say next or where the discourse is 'leading to';
— matching what we hear against our own experience, knowledge of the world, and preconceptions;
— trying to visualise elements of what we hear, and form a mental picture that corresponds roughly to that of the speaker;
— distinguishing the main point of what we hear from less important details, and 'following the thread' of a conversation or anecdote;
— listening out for particular points of detail that are especially relevant to us;
— responding intellectually and emotionally to what we hear: agreeing or disagreeing, approving or disapproving, being surprised, disturbed, amused, etc.
— inferring information about the speakers and their situation that is implied in what we hear.

We had these strategies very much in mind while developing the units that make up this book, and they are referred to in the *Map of the book* on pages 8–9. We have not regarded these strategies as discrete 'skills' that can or need to be taught; we have seen them rather as an underlying resource that students already have in their own language, and have tried to develop exercises which encourage students to draw on them to help them listen to English.

## The recordings

Natural spontaneous speech is quite different in its structure from scripted monologue or dialogue – as well as showing greater redundancy and often including more hesitation, there are important differences in rhythm and in the way speakers use pausing to divide up their message. Because of these differences, we feel that scripted recordings cannot adequately prepare students for listening to the natural language they will encounter in the real world. Consequently, nearly all the recordings for this book are of spontaneous, unscripted language; most of the material is taken from authentic informal interviews, while some is improvised by actors.

We have tried to include a variety of voices and speaking styles in the book, so that students have a chance to listen not only to 'standard British English' but also to a range of regional and other varieties of English. The recordings include speakers from Scotland, Ireland, Northern England, the United States and New Zealand, as well as speakers whose native language is Greek, German, Dutch and Spanish (in Units 5, 7, 13 and 17).

## Grading

Although we have selected recordings that do not have too heavy a lexical or structural load, we have avoided using 'simplicity of language' as our only criterion in grading the material. Instead, we have left the language as natural as possible and tried to incorporate other features into the book to bring the level down and make it accessible to intermediate learners:

– especially in the earlier units, the stretches of speech that students listen to at a time are kept quite short, and can easily be played several times over;
– longer pieces of listening are usually divided into shorter sections, each with its own listening task;
– in some units, isolated utterances have been rerecorded separately so that they can be listened to in isolation, either before or after the main listening activity; we hope that this helps to overcome the sense of panic that learners are liable to feel when listening to an apparently 'unstoppable' stream of language;
– in most of the recordings students only have to listen to one person speaking, although some units (e.g. 2A, 4A, 4B, 9A, 9B, 18A) intentionally introduce conversations between two or more speakers in order to focus on this as a comprehension feature;
– we have made extensive use of pre-listening activities, in which students are encouraged to make predictions about what they are going to hear. This not only helps to focus on the topic but it greatly simplifies the listening task by making the message more predictable.

# Using the book

## Structure of the book

Each unit is divided into two parts, A and B. Each part provides material for 30–45 minutes of class listening and associated activities. Usually the two parts of the unit are independent of each other, reflecting different aspects of one topic; in a few units (13, 14, 15, 17) the two parts develop a single idea and so belong more closely together. This structure is intended to make the material as flexible as possible: one part of any unit can be used on its own or the two parts can be used together.

## Listening in class

This book is mainly designed to be used in class, and this is reflected in the active approach we have taken to listening. Although the main focus of each unit is on listening, this is integrated into a range of oral (and sometimes written) activities. Each section begins with a pre-listening activity, to introduce the topic and prepare students for the listening; most of the listening tasks themselves are open-ended, to encourage students to discuss, comment, interpret and react, as well as merely record information; and the listening stage is followed by an extension activity in which students can use what they have listened to as a basis for creative speaking and writing.

## Self-study listening

Although the book is mainly intended for use in class, many of the activities can be done by students working alone with the cassette, either at home or in a self-access room or language laboratory, using the tapescript at the end of the book as an answer key. As each unit is divided into two sections, it would also be possible to cover the first half of each unit in class, and leave the second half for students to work through on their own outside class time.

We hope this book will help your students to listen to English effectively, and that both you and they enjoy using the material.

# Acknowledgements

The authors and publishers are grateful to the following for permission to reproduce copyright material.

Oslo Kommune Kunstsamlingene and Munchforlaget for 'The Scream' by Edvard Munch on p. 29; Harper Collins Publishers for the drawings on p. 33 from the *Collins Gem Guide to Mushrooms and Toadstools* by John Wilkinson and Stefan Buczacki, and for the drawings on p. 38 (top) from the *Collins Gem Guide to the Insects of Britain and Western Europe* by Michael Chinnery.

Photographs: Graham Bell (p. 11 left); University of Georgia (p. 11 right); Jeremy Pembrey (p. 17, p. 21); British Tourist Authority (p. 19 a, c); Edinburgh Photographic Library (p. 19 b); Bob Charnley (p. 28, photograph by Dr Smart), © copyright Bob Charnley Collection; Angus McBean/ Shakespeare Centre Library (p. 30); G. P. Corrigan/Robert Harding Picture Library (p. 43); Telegraph Colour Library (p. 44, p. 46, p. 47 left, p. 49 top); Colorsport (p. 47 middle); Action Plus (p. 47 right, by Chris Barry); Syndication International (p. 49 bottom).

Recording: The 'Flute et Koto du Japon' excerpt in Exercise 1A is courtesy of Musidisc and the Mechanical Copyright Protection Society Ltd; the excerpt from 'First of May' from *Never Die Young* by James Taylor in Exercise 1B is courtesy of James Taylor, Columbia Records and the Mechanical Copyright Protection Society Ltd.

Drawings by Julie Anderson, Helena Greene, Lisa Hall, Helen Herbert, Leslie Marshall and David McKee. Artwork by Hardlines and Peter Ducker. Book design by Peter Ducker MSTD.